# Toward a Theology of the Corporation

## Michael Novak

American Enterprise Institute for Public Policy Research
Washington and London

MICHAEL NOVAK is resident scholar in religion and public policy at the American Enterprise Institute and adjunct professor of religion at Syracuse University.

*The two chapters of this book were first delivered at two conferences in 1980, one held at the University of Notre Dame, the other jointly sponsored by the Syracuse University Department of Religion and the American Enterprise Institute. Both have been reworked and new materials added. The early version of the first chapter will appear in Oliver F. Williams and John W. Houck, eds.* The Judeo-Christian Vision and the Modern Business Corporation *(Notre Dame, Ind.: University of Notre Dame Press, 1981). An abridged version appeared under the title "God and Man in the Corporation," in* Policy Review *no. 13 (Summer 1980), pp. 9–32. The early version of the second chapter appears in the published proceedings of the Syracuse-AEI Summer Institute, Michael Novak and John W. Cooper, eds.,* The Corporation: A Theological Inquiry *(Washington, D.C.: American Enterprise Institute, 1981).* M.N.

**Library of Congress Cataloging in Publication Data**
Novak, Michael.
    Toward a theology of the corporation.

    (AEI studies ; 315)
    Bibliography: p.
    1. Business ethics. 2. Corporations—Moral and religious aspects. 3. Social values. I. Title. II. Series.
HF5387.N68    174'.4    81-1693
ISBN 0-8447-3432-2    AACR2

AEI Studies 315

5 7 9 10 8 6 4

*Printed in the United States of America*

# Contents

# Preface

Events in Iran and Nicaragua have begun to show public policy analysts that they omit religion—specifically, the ideas of theologians —from their calculations at their peril. Religion seems today to be as powerful a force in world affairs as at any time in the past; through modern instruments it may yet become more powerful than ever. So it is probably less necessary to persuade public policy experts to learn more about the intellectual activities of the world's religions than it is to persuade theologians and church leaders to attend more carefully, and more empirically, to matters of public policy. Before one can talk about the theology of the corporation, for example, one must learn a great deal about economics and political economy.

This book is intended to stimulate further debate not only among theologians but also among all who are interested in public policy, particularly as it bears on economics.

MICHAEL NOVAK
AEI Resident Scholar

# 1
## Can a Christian
## Work for a Corporation?

At first, I resisted mightily the title assigned to me: "Can a Christian work for a corporation?" Then I came to see a certain humor in it. Irving Kristol suggested the appropriate answer to the outrageous question: "No, only Muslims and Jews." Of course, a larger and more complicated answer is also necessary. To come to it, much preparatory work must first be accomplished by many theologians. Here I can barely make a beginning.

Few theologians have yet attempted to reflect systematically on economic activities and economic systems. Although mature theologies of history and fledgling political theologies do exist, there is as yet no theology of economics. In particular within the theology of economics there exists no theological description and critical evaluation of democratic capitalism. Most theologians of the last two hundred years have approached democratic capitalism in a premodern, precapitalist, predemocratic way; or else they have been socialists, usually romantic and utopian rather than empirical. Lacking both a theology of economics and a theology of democratic capitalism, it is difficult indeed to launch a third-order inquiry into the theology of the corporation.

The corporation is an invention of democratic capitalism, or, to put it another way, the corporation is an invention of law that made democratic capitalism possible. Neither participatory democracy nor capitalism could exist without the corporation. The existence and practice of the corporation, furthermore, give the lie to all theories of democracy and capitalism that focus exclusively on the individual to the neglect of human sociality. The corporation is an expression of the social nature of humans. Moreover, it offers a metaphor for the ecclesial community that is in some ways more illuminating than metaphors based on the human body ("the mystical body") or on the family, the clan, the tribe, or the chosen people.

Paul Johnson has pointed out that the corporation originated in the twofold need of religious communities, whose purpose transcends the life of the individual, for independence and self-subsistence.[1] Their motive was profit, in the sense that they needed to be sufficiently productive to have time for other things (prayer, honoring the dead) besides mere subsistence. They also needed independence and continuity over time. Pre-Christian religious communities in New Kingdom Egypt (around 1300 B.C.) owned property corporately, as did perpetual mortuary foundations in later Egyptian history. These Egyptian corporations influenced the incorporation of the late Roman Christian monastic communities, which benefited from the land deeds pioneered by late Roman law. The Benedictine monasteries, in turn, provided economic models for the lay guilds of the fourteenth and fifteenth centuries, and the guilds' legal structure was imitated by the merchant adventurers of the sixteenth century. These merchants then developed the joint stock company to raise capital and to share risks. Thence came the modern corporation—a communal institution whose purposes and continuity must transcend the limits of individual life. The lineage of the modern multinational corporation may likewise be traced in legal and economic history to the internationalism of the Benedictines and other general congregations of religious men and women. As leisure is the basis of culture, so profits exceeding the needs of subsistence underlay the economics of the independent, multinational religious orders. Often, to be sure, these self-sufficient congregations subsidized the time needed for prayer and study with the profits of their own excess productivity.

In a word, the modern economic corporation is a fruitful locus for theological inquiry, even though a full exploration of the theology of the corporation depends on a prior theology of democratic capitalism, which in turn depends on a prior theology of economics. Unfortunately, the necessary preliminary investigations cannot be set forth here; I hope to have an inquiry into such matters ready for publication in a year or two. The question addressed to me here is quite specific. It is also laden with denigrating bias.

Can a Christian work for a corporation? Under the logical paradigm for this question other vocations fall as well: Can a Christian

---

[1] Consultation at the American Enterprise Institute, April 2, 1980. See also Max Weber: "The modern rational organization of the capitalistic enterprise would not have been possible without ... the separation of business from the household. ... The indispensable requisites for this independence ... [include] our legal separation of corporate from personal property." *The Protestant Ethic and the Spirit of Capitalism*, trans. Talcott Parsons (New York: Charles Scribner's Sons, 1958), pp. 21–22.

work for the state? Can a Christian work in a university? Can a Christian be a bishop? Being a Christian is a high vocation—a vocation to grow in the holiness of Jesus Christ. Living before the age of democratic capitalism, Jesus did not work for a corporation. He did, apparently, work for a small business as a carpenter. His disciples, working as fishermen, appear to have been mostly independent small businessmen as well, and some presumably hired others to help them.[2] To be an economic animal is as much a part of human nature as to be a political animal or a religious animal. Indeed, human life is inconceivable apart from the economic activities necessary to create shelter, gather food, build roads, and establish markets.

A majority of lay Christians in approximately 30 of the world's 160 nations—including the United States, Japan, Hong Kong, Sri Lanka, and most nations of Western Europe—now live out their lives under systems at least reasonably analogous to democratic capitalism.[3] Democratic capitalism may be thought to have been distinguished fully from mercantilism with the publication of Adam Smith's *The Wealth of Nations* in 1776, and the founding of a "new order" in the United States. By "democratic capitalism," I mean a society no longer structured like a traditional society, in Max Weber's sense,[4] but rather differentiated into three social systems: a political system, an economic system, and a moral-cultural system. As the church is separated from

[2] "We shall view the [early] Christian movement ... not as a proletarian mass movement but as a relatively small cluster of more or less intense groups, largely middle class in origin." Robert M. Grant, *Early Christianity and Society* (New York: Harper & Row, 1977), p. 11.

[3] For a convenient analytic breakdown of the social systems of the world's 160 nations, consult the charts in Raymond D. Gastil, ed., *Freedom in the World* (New York: Freedom House, 1980), pp. 40-41.

[4] "A system of imperative coordination [authority] will be called 'traditional' if legitimacy is claimed for it and believed in on the basis that the sanctity of the order and the attendant powers of control as they have been handed down from the past 'have always existed.'" Max Weber, *The Theory of Social Economic Organization*, trans. A. M. Henderson and Talcott Parsons (New York: Free Press, 1947), p. 341. Weber contrasted "traditional" society with two other types, *charismatic* and *legal-rational*: "In traditionally stereotyped periods, charisma is the greatest revolutionary force.... It may ... result in a radical alteration of the central system of attitudes and directions of action with a completely new orientation of all attitudes toward the different problems and structures of the 'world'" (p. 363). "In legal [rational] authority, submission does not rest upon the belief and devotion to charismatically gifted persons, like prophets and heroes, or upon sacred tradition.... [It] is based upon an impersonal bond to the generally defined and functional 'duty of office.' The official duty ... is fixed by rationally established norms, by enactments, decrees, and regulations." Max Weber, "Social Psychology of the World's Religions," in H. H. Gerth and C. Wright Mills, eds., *From Max Weber* (New York: Oxford University Press, 1958), p. 299. See also David Little, *Religion, Order, and Law* (New York: Oxford University Press, 1969), chap. 2.

the state, so also the economic system is somewhat independent of the political system, and the reverse. If we are ever to have a credible theology of work, theology of the laity, and theology of the world, we will have to construct a sound fundamental theology of economics and a critical theology of democratic capitalism. For our present purposes, however, we will be obliged to focus attention upon the actual *praxis* of economic corporations, within which sizable numbers of Christians now perform their daily work and earn their daily bread.

The preliminary answer to the question, Can Christians work for a corporation? must therefore be: in fact many of them do. By corporation in this context is meant a legal body chartered and empowered by law to perform specifically designated functions under the restraint of law.[5] The existence of corporations depends on the evolution of a body of law; on such differentiation of society as permits corporations a certain independence from the state; and on freedom to enter into social contracts which constitute the corporation as a legal person and active agent in history.[6] In a more fundamental sense, corporations depend on at least an implicit metaphysics of "emergent probability," as Bernard Lonergan has defined it[7]; on the cultural evolution of notions of individual liberty, voluntary association, and formally free labor; and on the invention of systems of accounting, including double-entry bookkeeping.[8] Max Weber's reflections on these last points in *The Protestant Ethic and the Spirit of Capitalism* provide a preliminary survey of the social preconditions for the historical emergence of economic corporations.

[5] "The law is prone to emphasize that the corporation is a body chartered or recognized by the state; that it is a formal agreement, in the nature of a contract, among people joined in a common purpose; that it can hold property, contract, and sue and be sued in a common name; and that it has a length of life not subject to the lives of its members." Edward S. Mason, "Corporation," *International Encyclopedia of the Social Sciences*, vol. 3, p. 396. See also John P. Davis, *Corporations* (1905; reprinted, New York: Putnam, 1961); A. Berle and Gardiner C. Means, *The Modern Corporation and Private Property*, rev. ed. (New York: Harcourt Brace Jovanovich, 1968); Peter F. Drucker, *Concept of the Corporation* (New York: Day, 1946); Richard J. Barber, *The American Corporation* (New York: Dutton, 1970). Barber severely criticizes the corporation. By contrast, Robert Hessen argues that the state does not create corporations but only registers their "birth certificates." See *In Defense of the Corporation* (Stanford, Calif.: Hoover Institution Press, 1979).

[6] "Modern rational capitalism has need ... of a calculable legal system and of administration in terms of formal rules.... Such a legal system and such administration have been available for economic activity in a comparative state of legal and formalistic perfection only in the Occident." Weber, *Protestant Ethic*, p. 25.

[7] Bernard J. Lonergan, *Insight: A Study of Human Understanding*, rev. students' ed. (New York: Philosophical Library, 1965), pp. 121-28.

[8] Weber, *Protestant Ethic*, pp. 21-22.

Not all corporations are economic, of course. Political parties are incorporated, as are labor unions, universities, foundations, many charitable organizations, and many institutions of research, invention, science, and the arts. The development of corporate law opened human history to the action of social institutions freely entered into. Where they appear, these "mediating structures," which are larger than the individual but smaller than the state, make possible the flowering of human initiative, cooperation, and accountability.[9] They are of considerable historical significance. The traditions on which corporate law is based are not universal; not all Christians live under such traditions today. Is it good for Christianity that such corporations exist?

## Six Sources of Distortion

Some theologians today write as if corporations were evil forces and, indeed, as if democratic capitalism as a whole were incompatible with Christianity. In 1864 Pius IX enshrined an analogous view in his "Syllabus of Errors," declaring that same modern civilization to be incompatible with Catholicism. Declarations by church leaders and theologians on secular matters are always worth attending to, but those who issue them are not always as wise as they imagine. Insight into the organization of the secular world is not their strength. Even the most stalwart partisans can scarcely deny the great gap between the economic views of rank-and-file Christians and those of Christian leaders in the World Council of Churches, the National Council of Churches, and the Catholic Church's Peace and Justice Commission.[10]

[9] Peter L. Berger and Richard John Neuhaus, *To Empower People* (Washington, D.C.: American Enterprise Institute, 1977). Berger and Neuhaus specifically exclude the large corporations from their list of mediating structures, because their emphasis is on the smaller social institutions. However, if we include the criteria of both size and degree of public-vs.-private character, most large corporations and all small businesses would qualify as mediating structures. In my view, even the largest corporations are significant defenses against the power of the state. In an extended but real sense, General Motors is a mediating structure (it is smaller than the Lutheran Church), and its individual units are as much mediating structures as parishes are.

[10] Among representative documents one might consult, for Protestantism: the Oxford Conference (forerunner of the World Council of Churches), "Report on Church, Community, and State in Relation to the Economic Order," in J. H. Oldham, ed., *The Churches Survey Their Task* (London: Allen & Unwin, 1937); and the General Board of the National Council of the Churches of Christ in the United States of America, *Christian Concern and Responsibility for Economic Life*, February 24, 1966. For Catholicism: Joseph Gremillion, ed., *The Gospel of Peace and Justice* (Maryknoll, N.Y.: Orbis Books, 1976). Questions are raised about this theology by, among others, Ernest W. Lefever, *Amsterdam to Nairobi*

One explanation for this gap may be that the rank and file are less well educated and less knowledgeable about economics and Christianity than are the writers of ecclesiastical statements. Yet, given the rather broad distribution of education and experience among local clergy and laity today, such an explanation seems hardly convincing. An alternative explanation may be that church commissions are managed by a special social class of Christians with its own understandable bias.[11] What cannot be assumed in advance is that the writers of ecclesiastical documents have superior knowledge of economics and Christianity and their proper relation. Their views, too, must face relentless questions. Church leaders are more likely to err in this territory than in most others.[12] The gospel itself provides little guidance, as do theological traditions formed by traditional social orders. So church authorities have only a very weak authority, indeed, for their pronouncements in this area. Moreover, church leaders and theologians may be among the least experienced and trained of all Christians to speak about economic matters in modern societies.[13]

A theology of economics that wishes to be critical must, then, establish a point of view from which to submit to criticism all propositions, whatever their origin, about the relation of the Christian people to economics. A student of statements by church leaders and theologians on economic matters is likely to notice six specific kinds of ideology that recur without argument or justification.

**The Ideological Use of Poverty.** Poverty is highly praised in the Bible; so there is reason for church leaders to focus on it. But how? What is the meaning of "poverty"? What is its religious meaning? What is its economic meaning? When the Protestant Reformers

(Washington, D.C.: Ethics and Public Policy Center, 1979); Edward Norman, *Christianity and the World Order* (New York: Oxford University Press, 1979); Michael Novak, "Liberation Theology and the Pope," *Commentary* 67 (June 1979): 60-64, and "The Politics of John Paul II," *Commentary* 68 (December 1979): 56-61.

[11] For analogues see B. Bruce-Briggs, ed., *The New Class?* (New Brunswick, N.J.: Transaction Books, 1979). The notion of the new class was first employed by writers on the left: David T. Bazelon, *Power in America* (New York: New American Library, 1967); John Kenneth Galbraith, *The Affluent Society* (Boston: Houghton Mifflin, 1958), chap. 14; Michael Harrington, *Toward a Democratic Left* (New York: Macmillan Co., 1968), chap. 10. See also Michael Novak, "Needing Niebuhr Again," *Commentary* 54 (September 1972): 52-60.

[12] See Garry Wills, *Politics and Catholic Freedom* (Chicago: Regnery Co., 1964).

[13] This point was made to me recently by the provost of a major university, who cited in evidence the transcripts of students and faculty of the divinity school on campus. Few, he asserted, had rigorous intellectual training in economics or public policy.

slammed the monastery doors behind them, as Max Weber describes,[14] was ascetic poverty in the name of Christianity to be imposed upon the peoples of the world? Modern churchmen and theologians, oddly, seem to regard poverty not as a state to be praised but as a state to be eliminated. They often suggest that poverty is a scandal, that it is due chiefly to hardheartedness or to exploitation by the rich. They seldom distinguish among theories of poverty.[15] They seldom recount its historical dimensions, its universal persistence, or the methods by which, at some times and in some places, it has been alleviated. They use the concept ideologically, not empirically. They seldom seem to recognize, as J. L. Talmon does, how the ideological use of "poverty" lies at the origins of "democratic totalitarianism."[16] The attempt to justify Stalinism in the name of a promised future social justice is all too common.

Is poverty more widespread today than in the time of Jesus? Are rates of infant mortality higher? Is life expectancy lower? Is famine more common?[17] Are there greater disparities between rich

[14] "Asceticism, the more strongly it gripped an individual, simply served to drive him farther away from everyday life, because the holiest task was definitely to surpass all worldly morality. Luther . . . had repudiated that tendency, and Calvinism simply took this over from him. . . . Now every Christian had to be a monk all his life. . . . Those passionately spiritual natures which had formally supplied the highest type of monk were now forced to pursue their ascetic ideals within mundane occupations." Weber, *Protestant Ethic*, p. 121.

[15] See, e.g., P. T. Bauer, "Western Guilt and Third World Poverty," *Commentary* 61 (January 1976): 31-38.

[16] J. L. Talmon, *The Origins of Totalitarian Democracy* (Chicago: Praeger, 1960).

[17] Poverty and famine have been the perennial condition of mankind. There have been "over 750 famines spanning nearly six millenniums. . . . Mediterranean Europe was the region of highest famine occurrence in the 501 B.C.–A.D. 500 time period. Famines were recorded prior to 450 B.C., some lasting 20 years, but the first century A.D. was noted for disastrous famines. Thousands perished in the famine of A.D. 6. . . . Eastern Europe was the region of highest famine occurrence in the A.D. 1501–A.D. 1700 time period. . . . More than 150 famines were recorded here in a 200-year period. . . . Asia was the region of highest famine occurrence from 1701–1974. . . . The twentieth century has been the era of the great Russian/ USSR famines." Gary H. Koerselman and Kay E. Dull, eds., *Food and Social Policy I* (Ames, Iowa: Iowa State University Press, 1978), pp. 14-16. "The super-death-rate from acute famine and epidemics virtually disappeared during the 18th century in Western Europe because of agricultural advances, international trade that improved the availability of all resources, and better hygienic defenses (the famine of 1847 in Ireland was atypical)." "Population," *Encyclopaedia Britannica*, 15th ed. (Chicago: Encyclopaedia Britannica, 1977).

Citing E. Parmalee Prentice, *Hunger and History* (New York: Harper & Brothers, 1939), Henry Hazlitt writes: "The dwellings of medieval laborers were hovels—the walls made of a few boards cemented with mud and leaves. Rushes and reeds or heather made the thatch for the roof. Inside the houses there was a single room, or in some cases two rooms, not plastered and without floor, ceiling, chimney, fireplace or bed, and here the owner, his family and his animals lived

and poor than in the time of the Pharoahs and the Caesars? The sources of poverty may lie as much in nature and in culture as in economic structures. If the Kingdom of God in this world demands the elimination of poverty, it may also impose correlative demands on the production of wealth. Indeed, empirical and critical inquiry may suggest that the relevant intellectual problem is not poverty, which is widespread and immemorial, but how to produce wealth. If theologians are serious about poverty, they must develop an empirically founded theory about it.

**The World View of Traditional Societies.** Church leaders are tempted to think in terms appropriate to a traditional society rather than to a modern, differentiated, pluralist society.[18] Thus they are more likely to imagine that the economic order should be suffused with charity and justice from above or from some central focus.[19] They often

and died. There was no sewage for the houses, no drainage, except surface drainage for the streets, no water supply beyond that provided by the town pump, and no knowledge of the simplest forms of sanitation." Citing William Farr, "The Influence of Scarcities and of the High Prices of Wheat on the Mortality of the People of England," *Journal of the Royal Statistical Society* 9 (February 16, 1846), Hazlitt continues: "And, ever-recurring, there was famine: 'In the eleventh and twelfth centuries famine [in England] is recorded every fourteen years, on an average, and the people suffered twenty years of famine in two hundred years. In the thirteenth century the list exhibits the same proportion of famine; the addition of high prices made the proportion greater.' ... One writer has compiled a detailed summary of twenty-two famines in the thirteenth century in the British Isles, with such typical entries as: '1235: Famine and plague in England; 20,000 persons die in London; people eat horse-flesh, bark of trees, grass, etc.' (Cornelius Walford, "The Famines of the World," *Journal of the Royal Statistical Society* 41 [March 19, 1878]: 433.) Hazlitt summarizes Walford's data: "1005: famine in England. 1016: famine throughout Europe. 1064–72: seven years' famine in Egypt. 1148–59: eleven years' famine in India. 1344–45: great famine in India. 1396–1407: the Durga Devi famine in India, lasting twelve years. 1586: famine in England giving rise to the Poor Law system. 1661: famine in India; no rain fell for two years. 1769–70: great famine in Bengal; a third of the population—10 million persons—perished. 1783: the Chalisa famine in India. 1790–92: the Deju Bara, or skull famine, in India, so called because the dead were too numerous to be buried. This list is incomplete—as probably any list would be. In the winter of 1709, for example, in France, more than a million persons, according to the figures of the time, died out of a population of 20 millions." Henry Hazlitt, *The Conquest of Poverty* (New Rochelle, N.Y.: Arlington House, 1973), pp. 14-15.

[18] On conceptual differences in kinds of order, see Little, *Religion, Order, and Law*, chap. 1.

[19] "Free competition, however, though justified and quite useful within certain limits, cannot be an adequate controlling principle in economic affairs.... All the institutions of public and social life must be imbued with the spirit of justice, and this justice must above all be truly operative. It must build up a juridical and social order able to pervade all economic activity. Social charity should be, as it were, the soul of this order." Pope Pius XI, *Quadragesimo Anno*, para. 88.

imagine themselves to be prophets, utopians, or visionaries, improving society by their lights. Yet a modern social order must be pluralistic, permitting many different Christian, Jewish, Muslim, atheist, and other visions about its character. A modern social order necessarily regards church leaders as equal, but not privileged, participants in the common dialogue. Their visions of how justice and charity ought to be observed in the economic order do not, cannot, and should not determine the rules of the economic order, for others must also be free to work for their visions. The problem of order in a differentiated society has not been adequately addressed.

**Naiveté about Transfer Payments.** Led by the models of the Christian past that stressed paternalism and charitable giving, religious leaders are inclined to think that income gaps between humans are (a) unjust and (b) best eliminated by transfer payments.[20] In other words, those who have will better help the poor if they give of their abundance to the poor. This assumption is doubtful.[21] Supposing that gaps between poor and rich are immoral, it does not follow that transfer payments are the most practical method of equalizing incomes, or that their use promotes independence and self-sufficiency. The effectiveness of such a remedy must be demonstrated, not asserted.

**The Anticapitalist Bias of the Intellectuals.** Given the anticapitalist bias of the Roman Catholic Church, of major American and European Protestant theologians in this century, and of the pronouncements of the Protestant churches,[22] church leaders are vulnerable to systematic

[20] "Disturbing factors are frequently present in the form of the frightful disparities between excessively rich individuals and groups on the one hand and, on the other hand, the majority made up of the poor or, indeed, of the destitute.... Everything will depend on whether these differences and contrasts in the sphere of the possession of goods will be systematically reduced through truly effective means." Pope John Paul II, "John Paul II's United Nations Address," *The New York Times*, October 3, 1979. The Pope insisted in another talk in America that the wealthier nations should "give of their substance, not only of their plenty."

[21] "Foreign aid ... to underdeveloped countries ... has had far-reaching and sometimes brutal consequences, enormous costs, little success, and virtually no adverse criticism.... Economic achievement depends primarily on people's aptitudes and attitudes (e.g., interest in material success) and their social institutions and political arrangements ... not on handouts." P. T. Bauer, "Foreign Aid, Forever?" *Encounter* 42 (March 1974): 15, 17-18.

[22] There is already a small body of literature unmasking this ideology; yet much remains to be done. See Ludwig von Mises, *The Anti-capitalistic Mentality* (South Holland, Ill.: Libertarian Press, 1972); F. A. Hayek, ed. *Capitalism and the Historians* (Chicago: University of Chicago Press, 1954); Ernest van den Haag, *Capitalism: Sources of Hostility* (New Rochelle, N.Y.: Epoch Books, 1979); Michael Novak, ed., *The Denigration of Capitalism* (Washington, D.C.: American Enterprise Institute, 1979).

misperceptions about the nature of democratic capitalism. Few if any theologians or church leaders have set forth a theoretical understanding of democratic capitalism that is intended to be descriptively true. Commonly, they accept what Max Weber called "kindergarten" notions about the system.[23] Before describing it accurately, they are already adversarial to it. Many speak of "individualism," "acquisitiveness," "greed," "self-interest," "money," "success," and "competitiveness" as though these underlie the actual practice of democratic capitalism. For example, the Oxford Conference of 1937 described the system thus:

> When the necessary work of society is so organized as to make the acquisition of wealth the chief criterion of success, it encourages a feverish scramble for money, and a false respect for the victors in the struggle, which is as fatal in its moral consequences as any other form of idolatry.[24]

Do people in practice live this way? How many? A very great many people clearly do not. Perhaps theologians merely borrow from economists' descriptions of economic behavior. But economists note explicitly that they are speaking abstractly about "economic behavior" and "economic man," not about real persons enmeshed in the real social order. Because they commonly criticize economists for excessive abstraction, theologians themselves are bound to describe the real world of ordinary experience. For example, the basic institution of capitalism is the corporation—a social organism. Indeed, entire schools of criticism fault corporate life, not for an excess of individualism, but for an excess of social pressures toward conformism.[25] Church leaders are prone to rely on ideology rather than on an accurate phenomenological description of the forms of fraternity, sympathy, fellowship, and cooperation practiced in democratic capitalist societies, and in corporations.[26]

[23] "The impulse to acquisition, pursuit of gain, of money, of the greatest possible amount of money, has in itself nothing to do with capitalism.... It should be taught in the kindergarten of cultural history that this naive idea of capitalism must be given up once and for all." Weber, *Protestant Ethic*, p. 17.

[24] Oxford Conference, "Report on Church, Community, and State," pp. 104-05.

[25] See Sloan Wilson, *The Man in the Gray Flannel Suit*, new ed. (Cambridge, Mass.: Robert Bentley, 1979). See also the concept of the other-directed personality in David Riesman et al., *The Lonely Crowd* (New Haven, Conn.: Yale University Press, 1961).

[26] A few leads for further exploration are suggested in Michael Novak, *The American Vision: An Essay on the Future of Democratic Capitalism* (Washington, D.C.: American Enterprise Institute, 1978).

**Guilt Mongering.** The profession of church leaders and theologians requires them to criticize leaders of other institutions for falling short of religious ideals. But an economic order in a pluralist society cannot be based on the principles and ideals of any single church. It must instead be based on assumptions that permit all who participate to define their own values. Moreover, a just economic order in a pluralist society cannot be based solely on the concepts of virtue, innocence, and motivation taught by church leaders. The fact that democratic capitalism is based on *rational* self-interest[27] does permit Christians and Jews, rationally choosing their own vision of virtue and justice, to take part in it. But it does not permit such believers to impose on nonbelievers their own view of what is rational. A democratic capitalist economic order does *not* assume that human beings are depraved, motivated by self-interest, acquisitiveness, and greed. Operating from rational self-interest, defined as each participant chooses through faith, reason and virtue to define it,[28] many participants seek satisfactions from their work that are far from monetary, selfish, or materialistic. The social order is much enhanced by such choices. Philanthropy, the arts, education, research, and many other altruistic activities are expected to flower and do in fact flower under democratic capitalism.

**The Constantinian Temptation.** In traditional societies, church leaders (whether in Rome or in Geneva) were able to impose their own values on the entire civil society. It is difficult for church leaders to play such a role within a differentiated society. Thus there is often a secret hankering, a lingering nostalgia, for a planned society that would once again permit church leaders to be in alliance with civil leaders in suffusing an entire society with their values.[29] This new Constantin-

[27] "The impulse to acquisition . . . has in itself nothing to do with capitalism. . . . Capitalism *may* even be identical with the restraint, or at least a rational tempering, of this irrational impulse." Weber, *Protestant Ethic*, p. 17.

[28] "[Unlike Adam Smith] the Sentimental School assumed and asserted that there were natural and self-correcting limits to the pursuit of self-interest." Irving Kristol, "Adam Smith and the Spirit of Capitalism," in *The Great Ideas Today, 1976* (Chicago: Encyclopaedia Britannica, 1976), p. 289. Kristol quotes Adam Smith, *The Theory of Moral Sentiments* (pt. 3, chap. 1), who described the perfection of human nature as something far beyond self-interest, unless the latter is seen to include sympathy, benevolence, and altruism: "We endeavor to examine our own conduct as we imagine any other fair and impartial spectator would view it. . . . [It follows that] to feel much for others, and little for ourselves, that to restrain our selfish, and to indulge our benevolent affections, constitutes the perfection of human nature." See also Garry Wills, "Benevolent Adam Smith," *New York Review of Books*, February 9, 1978.

[29] The hidden premise in many discussions of the free market and of "private selfishness" is that public officials are by definition less selfish, more public-

ianism appears today as socialism in totalitarian states and as statism in mixed economies. Democratic capitalism functions as three systems in one, and it is altogether proper for leaders in the moral system or in the political system to place constraints on the economic system. But those constraints must be as jealously watched as those flowing in other directions, lest one of the three systems become excessively subordinated to another. Leaders in each system tend to manifest typical biases. Theologians and church leaders must learn to detect their own characteristic bias. If evangelical leaders tend to be biased toward economic leaders, liberal churchmen tend to be biased toward the state. Each such bias may be dangerous to the common health.

In the spirit of these warnings, let us turn now to some matters of fact about corporations in the United States.

## Some Observations on Matters of Fact

In order not to think of corporations in a merely mythical way, exaggerating their nature, scope, and relative position in society, it is important to grasp a picture of the factual context. Some of the numbers may be surprising to some readers. How many corporations are there in the United States? Some 2 million economic corporations now report to the Internal Revenue Service.[30] According to the Small Business Administration, there are an additional 13 million unincorporated small businesses.[31] (Since the active labor force in the United States numbers nearly 100 million persons, there is, on average, one business corporation for every six or seven workers.) Defined by the number of laborers employed by each enterprise, by the total assets of the enterprise, and by the annual sales volume of the enter-

---

spirited. Little in the history of state tryanny and state bureaucracy supports this premise. One must distinguish, further, two quite different types of rationality. One is the rationality that emerges as the calculus of individual choices in the market. The other is the rationality imposed by planners. Evidence suggests that, although neither form of rationality is complete, the former is more worthy of rational trust. Those who criticize the rationality of the market are usually utopian with respect to the rationality of planners. This is the new Constantinianism. A traditional Catholic culture like that of Latin America is especially prone to it. An alliance between commissars and clerics under "Christian Marxism" is a modern version of the imposition of a unitary moral vision on the political system and the economic system in a traditional society.

[30] U.S. Bureau of the Census, *Statistical Abstract of the United States, 1979* (Washington, D.C.: U.S. Department of Commerce, 1979), table 453.

[31] U.S. Small Business Administration, *Facts about Small Business and the U.S. Small Business Administration* (Washington, D.C.: U.S. Small Business Administration, n.d.), p. 1.

prise, there are approximately 15 million small businesses in the United States and about 700,000 large businesses.[32]

In recent years, the level of employment in industrial corporations has remained relatively static, or even declined, while the number of jobs in the service sector and in government employment has been growing rapidly. From 1969 to 1976, for example, nearly all the 9 million new jobs added to the economy were added in government employment (3 million) and in small businesses mostly in the service sector (6 million).[33] Employment in large businesses has been relatively static; the Small Business Administration claims that 87 percent of all new jobs in the private sector are created by small businesses.[34] Many of these small businesses, from rock groups to boutiques, spring up among young adults.

Of the approximately 100 million Americans who work, some 16 million civilians work for federal, state, and local governments. Another 4 million work under contract to the government.[35] In addition, all those on unemployment compensation, social security, and welfare depend on the state for income. Some 46 million of the workers in the private sector work for small businesses such as taxi fleets, local dairies and bakeries, retail stores, auto dealers, and restaurants.[36] The remainder, about 38 million, work for the estimated 700,000 large corporations, which thus employ on average 54 persons each. The New York Stock Exchange, the American Stock Exchange, and the Over-the-Counter market together list some 5,250 corporations whose shares are owned by the public and publicly traded. All these corporations rank as large businesses, although many of them employ only a few hundred workers.

Each year *Fortune* magazine lists the 500 largest industrial corporations in America. Over the years, corporations disappear and rankings change as new technologies spawn new giants and old technologies and methods of operation result in the decline or bankruptcy of others. For example, the tenth largest corporation, Chrysler, appears to some to be in its death throes. Within the *Fortune* 500, the

---

[32] Telephone interview with the chief economist at the National Small Business Association, March 21, 1980.

[33] Small Business Administration, *Facts*, p. 4.

[34] Telephone interview with an economist at the U.S. Small Business Administration, March 21, 1980.

[35] Bureau of the Census, *Statistical Abstract, 1979*, tables 509, 644. On consultants see Barbara Blumenthal, "Uncle Sam's Army of Invisible Employees," *National Journal*, May 5, 1979, p. 730.

[36] Small Business Administration, *Facts*, p. 3, and Bureau of the Census, *Statistical Abstract, 1979*, table 644.

top hundred are truly giants; the fifth hundred rank dramatically lower in net worth, annual gross sales, and numbers of employees.[37] Altogether, the top 500 corporations employ about 16 million Americans, about as many as those employed by the state, 4 million more than those who attend American colleges and universities as graduate students and undergraduates.[38] The average work force of the top 500 corporations is 28,000, approximately the number of students enrolled on the campuses of some major universities.

The smallest 200 of the *Fortune* 500 (by number of employees) employ under 13,000 persons each. The smallest of the 500 has only 592 employees. In other words, a majority of the *Fortune* 500 are of the size of universities, from 500 up to about 40,000 employees.[39] Running a multinational corporation in the *Fortune* 500 is, in most instances, about equivalent to running a major university. No corporation in the *Fortune* 500 has as many employees as the U.S. Department of Health, Education, and Welfare, counting its 800,000 full-time consultants. None has the number of employees of the Department of Defense, counting its civilian employees only. Only General Motors has more employees than the Postal Service. Table 1 contains these and other comparisons.

Most big corporations are smaller than many Roman Catholic dioceses: Syracuse has 421,023 Catholics, Brooklyn 1,415,662. The total employment of all the *Fortune* 500 companies (16 million) is smaller than the number of Baptists (25 million) and less than a third of the number of Catholics (50 million) in the United States. These corporations are also smaller than some national unions and smaller than many state universities.[40] The largest state university system, the State University of New York, had 41,000 full-time employees and 227,000 full-time students in fall 1979, for a total of 268,000

---

[37] In 1978 the top 100 firms held 67 percent of the assets of the *Fortune* 500, earned 66 percent of the net income, and employed 55 percent of the work force. The fifth 100 held 3 percent of the assets, earned 3 percent of the net income, and employed 5 percent of the workers. Bureau of the Census, *Statistical Abstract*, 1979, table 950.

[38] Ibid., tables 263, 509.

[39] "The Fortune Directory of the 500 Largest U.S. Industrial Corporations," *Fortune*, May 7, 1979, pp. 268-89.

[40] Members of the largest trade unions are as follows: Teamsters 1,889,000; United Auto Workers 1,358,000; United Steelworkers 1,300,000. See Bureau of the Census, *Statistical Abstract*, 1979, table 703. Employees of the largest universities are as follows: U.C.L.A., 55,937; University of Michigan, 45,723; University of Texas, 35,807; University of Wisconsin, 32,657. See Department of Health, Education, and Welfare, *Higher Education General Information Survey—Employees: Number and Characteristics and Salaries* (Washington, D.C.: National Center for Education Statistics, 1976).

## TABLE 1

### Seven Largest Organizations in Government and Business by Number of Employees

*U.S. Government*

| | |
|---|---|
| Executive Branch (total) | 2,806,513 |
| Dept. of Defense (civilians only) | 971,968 |
| U.S. Postal Service | 655,742 |
| Veterans Administration | 226,311 |
| Dept. of Health, Education, and Welfare | 163,230 |
| Dept. of Treasury | 130,873 |
| Dept. of Agriculture | 115,078 |
| Dept. of Interior | 77,465 |

*Fortune 500*

| | |
|---|---|
| General Motors | 839,000 |
| Ford Motor Company | 506,531 |
| General Electric | 401,000 |
| ITT | 379,000 |
| IBM | 325,517 |
| Mobil | 207,700 |
| U.S. Steel | 166,848 |

Sources: For government, U.S. Bureau of the Census, *Statistical Abstract of the United States, 1979* (Washington, D.C.: U.S. Dept. of Commerce, 1979), table 464. For corporations, "The Fortune Directory of the 500 Largest U.S. Industrial Corporations," *Fortune* (May 7, 1979), pp. 270-71.

(more than the employee total of the Mobil corporation or the U.S. Veterans Administration).[41]

Several other characteristics may be worth pointing out. These corporations are spread out over twenty-five industries, from aerospace to food processing to publishing.[42] Although there is some variation from industry to industry and from year to year, the companies' average annual return on investment in 1978 was 14.3 percent.[43] As frequently happens, the television industry led all others that year, with an annual return on investment of about 22 percent. Since it has been possible in recent years to get a return on investment of about 10 percent—lately, in an all-time peak, 15 percent—simply by putting one's money in the higher-ranked bank instruments, with virtually no risk, the incentive for investing capital in American industry is not at

[41] Telephone inquiry, Harry Charlton, Office of Institutional Research, Central Administration, State University of New York, November 26, 1980.
[42] Bureau of the Census, *Statistical Abstract, 1979*, table 951.
[43] Ibid.

present very high. Technological innovation is falling off; productivity is falling off dramatically. Since it requires about $30,000 of capital investment to create each new job, the drop in capital investment has limited job creation for several years.

Corporations are normally started by a few persons pooling their capital—often only a very little in the beginning, as when Hewlett and Packard began making electronic instruments in a small garage in Palo Alto, California, just after World War II—in order to bring some new idea to market. Practical insight is the first and indispensable constituent in the formation of a corporation; everything else depends on it. That idea cannot be realized in goods and services, of course, until someone puts up the money (capital in the secondary sense) to provide the instruments of manufacture and delivery. But money alone can be as easily lost as increased, invested productively as squandered. In addition to the money and prior to it is the *idea*, the organizing original *insight*. In their book *The Responsible Society*, Stephen B. Roman and Eugen Loebl have been among the most perspicacious in underlining the primacy of intelligence to the workings of democratic capitalism.[44]

Although large corporations have been important since the founding of America—whether the British companies that founded early colonies or the organizations involved in hunting and transportation, canal building, and railroads—they did not become a conspicuous part of the American landscape until after the Civil War and, even more so, after the creation of a national, transcontinental society in the twentieth century.[45] From the Revolutionary War, at least, Americans properly feared the large, all-encompassing state. For the last century, this fear of bigness has been redirected at the growing number of large corporations. General Motors, the giant among corporations with 839,000 employees, is much smaller than the federal government. Still, a single corporation employing more persons than are to be found in several of our states is a formidable economic force. Most large corporations are far smaller than General Motors. Of the *Fortune* 500, 419 have under 50,000 employees each, 300 have under 23,000 employees each, and the fifth 100 have under 8,200 employees

[44] Stephen B. Roman and Eugen Loebl, *The Responsible Society* (New York: Regina Ryan Books/Two Continents, 1977).

[45] "The forces that made this industrial growth possible were released by the Civil War, but they were bound in any event to have made their influence felt." Foster Rhea Dulles, *The United States since 1865* (Ann Arbor, Mich.: University of Michigan Press, 1959), p. 52. Most historians write rather negatively of business and the corporations in the United States. Scholars should perhaps reconsider the evidence in the light of the prevalence of anticapitalist bias, so that the evidence may speak for itself.

each. Yet even the smallest of the 500 (592 employees) faces enormous problems of innovation, continued vitality, and organization in order to function at all.[46] If one considers the problems of financing, management, quality, and morale in the running of a large university, or—at the other extreme—the problems of managing the truly gigantic work forces of the government, one may be able to appreciate the appropriate scale of corporate management. The vast majority of corporations are smaller than our large universities.

It is a common mistake to believe that almost anyone can manage a large corporation and to underestimate the relative scarcity of high talent. Literary intellectuals (including theologians) tend to value a type of intelligence, important for its own sake but not necessarily adequate to the demands of economic management.[47] Indeed, the sort of work intellectuals value most highly is often unlikely to be successful in the market. Their way of thinking, then, has a natural affinity to aristocratic rather than to commercial ideals. In much of our work we reject the standards of the market in preference for judgments made in the light of intrinsic values of traditional weight.[48] We tend to think that persons of industry and commerce exercise vulgar judgment. Yet creative practical intelligence must also go against the market; it claims to change the market. An economic system like ours rewards such dissent, anticipation, and innovation. It also penalizes mistaken strategic decisions, which can threaten to bankrupt even the tenth largest company, Chrysler. At the time when corporate decisions must be made, it is not at all certain which of competing decisions will be the correct one. Practical intelligence of a high order is often obliged to fight its way through legions of doubters who "know" from the conventional wisdom that novel proposals cannot work.

Lenin once expressed the view that any citizen could manage the government, hence a socialist economy, just as any one of them could in a short time be trained to work as a postal clerk. Moreover, folklore is full of "robber barons," "fat cats," "tycoons," and images of hereditary wealth and financial control, dating from an era prior to the

---

[46] "The Fortune Directory of the 500 Largest Industrial Corporations."

[47] See Lonergan's discussion of insight in various forms of common sense and its systematic biases. *Insight*, chaps. 6 and 7.

[48] "The intellectual's hostility to the businessman presents no mystery, as the two have, by function, wholly different standards, so that the businessman's normal conduct appears blameworthy if judged by the criteria valid for the intellectual's conduct.... The businessman offers to the public 'goods' defined as anything the public will buy; the intellectual seeks to teach what is 'good,' and to him some of the goods offered are things of no value which the public should be discouraged from wanting." Bertrand de Jouvenal, "The Treatment of Capitalism by Continental Intellectuals," in Hayek, ed., *Capitalism*, pp. 116-118.

managerial revolution. Corporate executives normally do not own the corporations they manage.[49] They are hired professionals, often of uncommon talent, and relatively mobile. The average length of service of a chief executive officer is about that of a professional football player: six years. The pay—in the *Fortune* 500 it averages $400,000 per year—is about commensurate with that of top professionals in sports, entertainment, television journalism, or writers of best-sellers. It is rarely as dramatic as that of some television and movie producers, inventors, and others. About 3 percent of the 77 million American households receive a one-year income in excess of $50,000. Only 275,000 persons, on average 5,500 in each of the fifty states, receive a one-year income in excess of $100,000.[50] (Certain academic authors of widely used textbooks are to be found in this number.)

The imagery surrounding corporate leaders is mainly negative; it seems to be inspired ideologically (and even ethnically). Few people write or talk about "fat cat" professors or journalists, athletes or actors, surgeons or lawyers, whose incomes are comparable or higher. In *The View from Sunset Boulevard*, Ben Stein has reproduced interviews that dramatize quite starkly the antibusiness attitudes of the makers of television and the ideological distortions of their perceptions.[51]

In the American past the "huddled masses" had reason to regard the "robber barons" as their class, ethnic, and even religious enemies. Such passions have continued in more moderate form into the present. Religious and ethnic resistance to Catholics and Jews in major corporations seems to have persisted until after World War II, but it has largely collapsed under the onslaught of talented professional managers like Thomas A. Murphy of General Motors, Lee Iacocca of Chrysler, Irving Shapiro of du Pont, and many others.

Rather distinct from the class of professional managers is the smaller class of corporate executives who built or helped build corporations around their own inventions or insights. Such persons commonly benefit not only from salaries but also from their substantial interest in the company. Indeed, building a company, even a small company like an auto dealership or a small chain of retail stores, is a'

[49] Berle and Means, *Modern Corporation.* See also Crawford H. Greenewalt, *The Uncommon Man: The Individual in the Organization* (New York: McGraw-Hill, 1959).

[50] U.S. Bureau of the Census, *Household Income in 1977* (Washington, D.C.: U.S. Department of Commerce, 1977), p. 1. Bureau of the Census, *Statistical Abstract, 1979,* table 442.

[51] Ben Stein, *The View from Sunset Boulevard* (New York: Basic Books, 1979), chap. 4.

far surer path to wealth than working as a professional manager.[52] Ownership in the firm enables the owner to accumulate wealth as capital; it is not paid him in salary. The limousine service from New Haven, Connecticut, to La Guardia and Kennedy airports was sold recently by its founder, for example, for a reported $13 million.

The largest industries are in almost all cases the most heavily unionized. Their businesses usually pay the best pension benefits, medical benefits, vacation benefits, and the rest. Smaller businesses rarely have the cash flow, security, or permanence to do nearly as well.

In an interdependent world, economic enterprises—like churches, scientific associations, and other institutions—have become multinational. Within the United States, American firms compete with multinational corporations founded and based in other lands: British Petroleum, Volvo, Sony, Olivetti, Volkswagen, and many others. In 1970 the Department of Commerce surveyed 298 U.S. firms with operations overseas.[53] Sperry Lea and Simon Webley note that, under a stricter definition of the term, there are only about 200 multinational corporations based in the United States, out of 300 worldwide.[54] These U.S. firms make roughly two-thirds of their sales in the developed countries and one-third in developing countries. Only a small fraction of total U.S. economic activity is involved in the developing world.

Multinational corporations encounter many moral dilemmas in doing business overseas. In most traditional societies bookkeeping is not public, nor bound solely by law. Custom and tradition have a

---

[52] In describing corporate wealth, socialists commonly fail to distinguish newcomers to wealth from older families of wealth. In each generation new fortunes are being made (McDonald's, Xerox, Polaroid, Texas Instruments), as new technologies are invented and new services organized, while fortunes based on obsolete technologies are often dissipated. Downward mobility is an important feature of the system, and may have only a slightly smaller frequency than upward mobility. There is also a fascinating circulation of elites in all three systems (economic, political, moral-cultural). Each generation of successful people, moreover, has great difficulty in passing on its talents, skills, drive, motivation, and success to the next generation. It is easier to give children every advantage money can buy than to pass on qualities of intelligence and character.

[53] U.S. Bureau of Economic Analysis, *Special Survey of U.S. Multinational Companies, 1970* (Washington, D.C.: U.S. Bureau of Economic Analysis, 1970).

[54] "Strictly speaking, MNCs [multinational corporations] comprise only a relatively few of the swelling number of firms operating internationally. Investigators have developed meaningful distinctions on the basis of such criteria as size, the importance and geographic spread of foreign operations, and the locus of decision making. In very round numbers, only about 300 firms—of which 200 are American—qualify as bona fide MNCs by the tighter definitions." Sperry Lea and Simon Webley, *Multinational Corporations in Developed Countries: A Review of Recent Research and Policy Thinking* (Washington, D.C.: British-North American Committee, 1973), p. 1.

familial base.[55] Ruling families consider it a right, perhaps a duty, to take a percentage of all commercial transactions, much as the governments of developed states levy taxes. In developed societies such extralegal but customary and traditional payoffs are considered bribes and are both illegal and immoral. The effort by Americans to impose American standards of commercial behavior on foreign authorities is not regarded as wise in all nations. Moral conflicts are inevitable in an interdependent world whose systems of law and morality are not as interdependent as its economic activities.

Favored by nature, the United States depends on foreign trade for relatively few commodities. It depends heavily on foreign oil, although some argue that the nation should long ago have cut its use of foreign oil to a small fraction of its present proportion. The United States is even more dependent on specialty metals like chromium, titanium, and a score of others that are indispensable to advances in high technology.[56] In addition, some U.S. industries, especially high-technology industries like aerospace but also agriculture, depend heavily on exports. In both imports and exports, then, the U.S. economy is interdependent with the world economy. Would those who oppose multinationals simply ban them? This can be and has been done. No multinational corporation is as strong as a state, which has an army and can restrict and tax corporations as it will. Even small states have confiscated the properties of major corporations and banned such corporations from their territory. Thus many corporations refuse to do business overseas except under unusually stable conditions.

Meanwhile, accusations against the activities of U.S. corporations abroad demand case-by-case intelligent judgment.[57] No doubt corporations are often wrong. No doubt they have been unprepared for the complexities of their interaction with host cultures, finding that methods and attitudes suited to the United States can have unfortunate effects abroad. Yet the absence of investment from abroad may be more morally damaging to traditional societies than is the activity of multinational corporations. The clash between modern and traditional societies would be ridden with moral conflict under the most favorable conditions.

[55] See Jeane Kirkpatrick, "Dictatorships and Double Standards," *Commentary* 68 (November 1979): 44.

[56] James F. McDivitt and Gerald Manners, *Minerals and Men*, rev. ed. (Baltimore: Johns Hopkins University Press, 1974), pp. 59-62.

[57] See, e.g., Richard J. Barnet and Ronald E. Muller, *Global Reach: The Power of the Multinational Corporations* (New York: Simon & Schuster, 1974). Cf. Ralph K. Winter, *Government and the Corporation* (Washington, D.C.: American Enterprise Institute, 1978), chap. 3; and Barber, *American Corporation*.

One thing is certain: Democratic capitalism needs to attend as much to cultural systems as to economic and political systems. On these matters, theologians may have something to contribute; but it would be arrogant to think that we, like Solomon, can resolve all perplexities. Should corporation X invest in a new plant in under-developed nation Y? Does it have the human resources to do so with cultural wisdom? What ought a Christian corporate executive to consider in making such a decision? We do not at present, I fear, offer much light.

Why not?

## Elements of a Theology of Economics

Theologians have little to say about the practical dilemmas of corporate executives for several reasons, but one significant reason is that the theology of economics is at present the least sophisticated branch of theological inquiry. Few theologians who address the social order (for example, Juergen Moltmann today or Paul Tillich a generation ago) have paid extensive attention to economic matters. The official documents of the popes and of Protestant ecumenical bodies (the World Council and the National Council) are notably strong on moral vision, much less so in describing economic principles and realities. The coming generation will inherit as a task the need to create and to set forth systematically a theology of economics that deals critically with several key concepts such as those that follow.

**Order.** There is a difference between the way a traditional society orders the cosmos of human meaning (political, economic, moral) and the way a modern democratic, pluralistic, capitalist society orders meaning.[58] To judge modern democratic, pluralistic, capitalist societies by the norms of traditional societies is to apply an inappropriate category. Those who do so often falsely describe the risk, danger, and terror inherent in personal liberty ("the experience of nothingness"[59]) under pejorative notions like alienation, anomie, and privatization. Order in a nontraditional society necessarily seems like disorder to those whose ideal is the order of a traditional society, as illustrated by the resentment of modernity among Iranian traditionalists. Socialist societies like Cuba, the U.S.S.R., and China offer a single system of meaning ("justice") far closer to that of traditional societies than to that of a fully differentiated modern society.

[58] See Little, *Religion, Order, and Law,* chap. 1.
[59] Michael Novak, *The Experience of Nothingness* (New York: Harper & Row, 1970).

**Emergent Probability.** Many theologians are fascinated by the future, by utopian thinking, by prophecy, and by the myth of the avant-garde. Moreover, the phrase "the economy of salvation" suggests to some that history moves forward by a kind of moral imperative (and inexorable necessity) toward self-improvement. By contrast, a theology of economics requires a critical philosophy of history. A promising candidate appears to be the theory of "emergent probability" sketched by Bernard Lonergan:[60] a world order moved neither by necessity alone nor by human will alone, neither wholly open to intellectual insight nor wholly closed to it, neither guaranteeing that the future will be better than the present nor ruling out all hope of some improvement. A theology of emergent probability contrasts with Moltmann's theology of hope.[61]

**Sin.** Any social order that intends to endure must be based on a certain realism about human beings and, therefore, on a theory of sin and a praxis for dealing with it. However sin is defined, its energies must be given shape, since sinful energies overlooked in theory are certain to find outlets in practice. Thus some hypothesize that democratic capitalism is based on self-interest, greed, acquisitiveness, egotism.[62] Others hypothesize that socialism—particularly in its egalitarianism—is based on envy and resentment.[63] Since no realistic social order can be based on expectations of heroic or even consistently virtuous behavior, it seems that a realistic social order must be designed around ideals rather lower than Christian ideals. Particularly

[60] Lonergan, *Insight*, chaps. 6 and 7.

[61] See Juergen Moltmann, *Theology of Hope* (New York: Harper & Row, 1967).

[62] R. H. Tawney is typical in this regard: "The quality in modern societies which is most sharply opposed to the teaching ascribed to the Founder of the Christian Faith . . . consists in the assumption . . . that the attainment of riches is the supreme object of human endeavor and the final criterion of human success. . . . Compromise is as impossible between the Church of Christ and the idolatry of wealth, which is the practical religion of capitalist societies, as it was between the Church and the State idolatry of the Roman Empire." R. H. Tawney, *Religion and the Rise of Capitalism* (New York: New American Library, 1926), pp. 234-35. In contrast to Tawney, Milton and Rose Friedman write: "Narrow preoccupation with the economic market has led to a narrow interpretation of self-interest as myopic selfishness, as exclusive concern with immediate material rewards. Economics has been berated for allegedly drawing far-reaching conclusions from a wholly unrealistic 'economic man' who is little more than a calculating machine, responding only to monetary stimuli. That is a great mistake. Self-interest is not myopic selfishness. It is whatever it is that interests the participants, whatever they value, whatever goals they pursue." Milton and Rose Friedman, *Free to Choose* (New York: Harcourt Brace Jovanovich, 1980), p. 27.

[63] See Helmut Schoeck, *Envy*, trans. Michael Glenny and Betty Ross (New York: Harcourt, Brace & World, 1969); and Leszek Kolakowski, *Main Currents in Marxism*, 3 vols. (New York: Oxford University Press, 1978), esp. the epilogue.

in a pluralist social system, the rules should not be so defined that every participant must, in effect, be a practicing Christian. (It is possible but not likely that Christian rules might be arrived at consensually.)

**Practical Wisdom.** The practical world depends as much on insight and intelligence as does the intellectual world. Certainly the economic system does. The role and conditions of insight in particular societies need close and concrete study.

**The Individual.** The most distinctive contribution of Judaism and Christianity to social theory is the identification of the individual conscience as a major source of social energy. Not all energy comes from authority, as the ancients held; nor from social structures, as the Marxists hold; nor from historical necessity; nor from class struggle. The individual is an originating source of insight, decision, and action.

**Community.** Human experience is by destiny familial. Primordially, it has been centered in family, clan, tribe, people. As the institutions of social organization have become differentiated, human sociality has also moved outward into an array of institutions: government agencies, political parties, unions, corporations, factories, schools and universities, diverse churches, associations, and others. In the economic sphere today sociality seems far more prevalent than individualism. In democratic capitalist nations various social organisms, including the business enterprise and the corporation, have replaced or supplemented old loyalties to family and clan. Some persons today are closer to their colleagues in the workplace than to their family. The business corporation is a relatively new organism in social history. It is perhaps the best secular analogue to the church, which is also often incorporated. Both are legal persons, unitary beings, constituted by voluntary contract, animated by social purposes, and subject to pervasive disciplines. The community and sociality that corporations make possible within themselves and in the surrounding social field deserve concrete description.

**Distribution.** The classic moralist's principle for the economic order is distributive justice. For traditional societies, which had no moral decision to make about growth, distributive justice was a first principle. Such societies were mostly static with a finite and already known supply of worldly goods, so traditional ethicists properly concentrated on how the store of goods ought to be distributed. Until the rise of democratic capitalism a permanent condition of poverty was seen as a given. Indeed, in the 1780s four-fifths of all French families spent 90 percent of their income simply buying bread—only bread—to stay alive. In 1800 fewer than 1,000 people in the whole of Germany had incomes as high as $1,000. Yet in Great Britain from 1800 to 1850, after the sudden capitalist take-off that had begun in 1780, real wages quadrupled, then quadrupled again between 1850 and 1900.[64] The world had never seen anything like it. After World War II dozens of other nations—but not all nations—used the ideas of democratic capitalism to experience even more rapid growth. The fact that economic growth has suddenly become a matter of human freedom has made moral decisions about growth and productivity prior, both logically and practically, to questions of distribution. What is not produced cannot be distributed, and choices about production condition choices about distribution.

**Scarcity.** The current lively debate about the limits of growth—recently summarized brilliantly by Seymour Martin Lipset[65]—involves three separate issues. One is a question of fact and empirical probability, and here the critics of the Club of Rome seem to be gaining the upper hand. The second concerns the role of technology and science. It seems odd, so soon after the disastrous struggles between religion and science in preceding generations, that many theologians such as Juergen Moltmann[66] should be trying to enlist the Christian church in opposition to growth. The resistance to growth is doubly odd, since technology and science can yet turn in many new directions, depending largely on the wisdom, needs, and investments of individuals and societies. Slowdowns in some directions do not entail slowdowns in others. The third issue in the debate over growth concerns the basis of democratic capitalism. Some people hold that it is grounded on an assumption of plenty, but nothing could be further from the truth. As Peter Clecak shows, the distributive ethics of socialism do depend on economic abundance and become irrelevant under conditions of scarcity.[67] A market system, by contrast, is

[64] Paul Johnson cites these numbers in *Will Capitalism Survive?* ed. Ernest W. Lefever (Washington, D.C.: Ethics and Public Policy Center, 1979), pp. 4-5. See also his *Enemies of Society* (New York: Atheneum, 1977).
[65] Seymour Martin Lipset, "Predicting the Future of Post-industrial Society," in *The Third Century*, ed. Seymour Martin Lipset (Stanford, Calif.: Hoover Institution Press, 1979), pp. 1-35.
[66] See Juergen Moltmann's comments on economic growth in *The Church in the Power of the Holy Spirit* (London: SCM Press, 1977).
[67] Peter Clecak, *Crooked Paths* (New York: Harper & Row, 1977), pp. 153-55.

designed to deal efficiently with either scarcity or abundance. A no-growth, limited economy of scarcity is not at all incompatible with a market system; scarce items have long been allocated by markets. Scarcity can impose cruel dilemmas, but it does not make democratic capitalism impossible. Indeed, democratic capitalism—and modern economies—were invented as methods for escaping the Malthusian trap of scarcity.

## Democratic Capitalism and the Corporation

Although space does not allow a section on the theology of democratic capitalism, a few words of elucidation are nonetheless necessary. For to encourage young Christians and Jews to turn their idealism and longing for service to the corporate world, without at the same time offering them a reason why democratic capitalism is theologically acceptable or even good, would be to plunge them into bad faith. Put with exquisite succinctness, that reason is the connection, in practice and in theory, between political liberty, or human rights, and democratic capitalism.

Even those monks of old who washed dishes, did the laundry, swept the floors, pruned the living vines in the vineyards, milked the cows, or copied manuscripts in tedious labor knew that they served the Kingdom of God and the liberation of humankind. So also it is with the contemporary laborer, however humble, in the contemporary corporation, however modest or even frivolous its product. To serve human needs, desires, and rational interests is also to serve human liberty, conscience, and God. Only if we can make an affirmative theological judgment about democratic capitalism can we develop a plausible theology of the lay world and a theology of work. Without such an affirmative judgment no one is in good faith except those determined to destroy an evil system.

In this respect, the Freedom House charts of the 160 nations of the world graphically dramatize a fact that is slowly becoming well known: There are no socialist states that are also democratic.[68] Political liberty and economic liberty are, de facto, closely related. Human rights seem to depend on a differentiated system in which the economic system is relatively free, the political system is relatively free, and the moral-cultural system is relatively free. The relationship appears to be theoretical as well as factual, for it is difficult to see

---

[68] "Freedom is directly related to the existence of multiparty systems: the further a country is from such systems, the less freedom it is likely to have." Gastil, *Freedom in the World, 1980*, p. 42.

how a political system can be free if individuals are not free to make their own economic decisions. If printing presses are not free of government economic controls, for example, it is not likely that ideas can circulate freely. Indeed, the Polish government maintains totalitarian control less by the use of police and armies (although these are abundant there) than by total legal control over wages, prices, interest, contracts, and every other aspect of economic behavior.[69] Economic totalitarianism is constituted by total public control and total public accountability.

Under democratic capitalism accountability must be clearly distinguished from subordination. The churches must not, through institutional controls, be made subordinate to the state in their decisions of conscience. The political system must not be subordinated to economic institutions. The economic system must not become subordinate to the political or religious system. To return to state or church control over economic behavior would be to return to mercantilism or, as Weber called it, "patrimonial" capitalism: a collapsing of the tripartite differentiation of the economic, the political, and the moral-cultural systems. The three interdependent but autonomous systems of democratic capitalism are accountable to each other and to the citizens through whom each has its historical existence. But no one of them can be permitted to become subordinate to the other two.

Short of subordinating the other two to itself, each of the three systems may properly, and often must, criticize the other two, inject new ideas into them, and impose many legitimate sanctions on them. Laissez faire is impermissible for any of the three systems. Those of us who believe in a strong state, active even in the economic sphere, must be especially alert to the dangers of confusing accountability with subordination. A great deal can be accomplished through persuasion, public criticism, and public protest. Each of the three systems is vulnerable to public opinion, for each depends for its daily functioning on a good reputation and a favorable climate of ideas. Each must appeal to voluntary support from citizens who are free to choose against them. Each must be accountable to its own internal system and, on the basis of autonomy and equality, to the other two systems from which it has been differentiated while by no means being invested with carte blanche.

Utopian theories of liberty are out of place in the real world. No perfectly free, just, or rational society ever has existed or ever

---

[69] I visited Poland for the first time from November 17 to December 5, 1979, and described this point in "A Lesson in Polish Economics," *Washington Star*, December 15, 1979.

will exist. This fact and this expectation are wholly consistent both with Christian conceptions of original sin and with the nonutopian liberal political philosophies of the West. Democratic capitalism is not without sin. Yet no one can plausibly claim that the tripartite system of democratic capitalism is inferior in its political liberties, broad distribution of benefits, and productive achievements to any historical alternative yet experienced by the human race. The system need not fear empirical comparisons with traditional and socialist societies.

The largest proportion of American workers, among them many Christians and Jews, work for small corporations. In so doing, the workers build the material economic base on which a society of liberty depends for its political and cultural liberties. Another large proportion of Christians and Jews work for so-called large corporations, most of which are actually modest in size. These workers, too, serve liberty as well as their own rational self-interest. About 16 million Americans work for the *Fortune* 500 corporations, and of these some 8.8 million work for the hundred largest corporations. Although these giants carry with them the dangers of great size, their size is absolutely essential to the task set before them: The airliners that carry most of us to meetings could not have been built by small corporations. Nor would such corporations be less dangerous if they were owned and operated by the state. Indeed, it is almost certain that if owned by the state, such corporations would perform far less humanely and far less efficiently than at present—and would also run deficits. Those with experience of government-owned and government-controlled enterprises have observed the morale and performance prevalent in such industries.

What Christians and Jews who labor for large corporations most lack is an intellectual and moral theory that (1) expresses the high spiritual vocation their work serves; (2) articulates the ideals of democratic capitalism so that they can judge and improve on their present practice; and (3) provides concrete guidance in the many decisions they must reach every day. Executives have considerable discretion over their decisions. With a set of principles and case studies, they could tilt many of their decisions to align them better with the ideals of the moral-cultural system that is so important to the tripartite system by which we live. Such executives are played false by moral-cultural leaders who misunderstand the ideals of democratic capitalism and who manifest so much naiveté and utopianism about government officials.

Although moral-cultural leaders speak earnestly about the need for accountability in the economic system, they do not yet appear to think clearly about the consequences of vesting such accountability in the state. Ethicists do not yet balance their analysis of the moral dangers of selfishness, immorality, and corruption in the economic system with a parallel analysis of the moral dangers of selfishness, immorality, and corruption in the political system.[70] The public interest is best served by an economic system powerful enough to resist and to restrain the political system, for the classic danger to liberal ideals comes far more from the tyranny of the public sector than from the sins of the private sector. Scholars determined to be as neutral as possible between the large corporations and the state must, in fairness, begin to analyze the specific lack of accountability, the specific corruptions, and the specific evils endemic to the public sector, as they already analyze those of the private sector.

I advise intelligent, ambitious, and morally serious young Christians and Jews to awaken to the growing dangers of statism. They will better save their souls and serve the cause of the Kingdom of God all around the world by restoring the liberty and power of the private sector than by working for the state. I propose for the consideration of theologians the notion that the prevailing moral threat in our era may not be the power of the corporations but the growing power and irresponsibility of the state.

The health of the Christian church and the Jewish people in the next century will depend to an extraordinary degree on the perspicacity of the present generation in discerning where the greater danger lies, and in throwing its weight with the weaker party. Merely to follow the conventional wisdom on these matters would be to betray the unrestricted drive to understand.

### The Praxis of Democratic Capitalism

It would be intellectually unsatisfying to leave this subject without making some comments on the moral practice that flows from the theology of the corporation outlined so briefly above. Since democratic capitalism is a tripartite system, it is wrong to think of it merely as a free-enterprise system. The economic system is only one of three systems, each of which has claims on our loyalty, each of which is indispensable for the functioning of the others. Although there is much to be gained when the leaders of each system respect the relative autonomy of the other two, and when each system fulfills its own specific responsibilities first, no one of these three systems

---

[70] See Charles Wolf, Jr., "A Theory of Non-market Failures," *The Public Interest* 55 (Spring 1979): 114-33.

stands alone. Each of us human beings is at once a citizen of a democracy, an economic worker, and a moral agent within a culture. Not only is it possible for an economic system to be suffused with moral purpose and religious belief, Max Weber argued that democratic capitalism is distinct from other commercial systems in the world *because of* the religious and moral value it attaches to commerce. It is one thing to tolerate commerce and to regard it as a vulgar necessity. It is another to regard it as the fulfillment of a vocation from God and a way of cooperating in the completion of Creation as God intended it.

To be sure, a fully differentiated type of democratic capitalism cannot impose a religious vocation and a religious self-understanding on all who partake in it. Pluralism requires openness to other motivations and understandings. There are in all cultures and at all times persons who believe that power and wealth are the actual goals of striving, despite moralists' insistence on the importance of virtue and high-mindedness. If the belief did not persist, the dialogues of Socrates and Thrasymachus and the dialectical arguments of Aristotle about the nature of true happiness would have no relevance for the ages.

In their useful little casebook, *Full Value*, Oliver F. Williams and John W. Houck give two categories of moral flaw often cited by a public that is losing confidence in the moral integrity of business: "1. numerous violations of legal codes that have come to the attention of the public, such as price fixing, tax law violations, and bribery. 2. breaches of the professional code of ethics by business persons, such as deceptive advertising, selling company secrets, and dishonesty in expense accounts."[71] These problems are immemorial; no system will ever eliminate them. They are encountered, analogously, in politics, government service, the academy, and other professions. Yet every immorality must be struggled against. Williams and Houck quite successfully juxtapose the power of the Christian story, in its biblical immediacy, to concrete problems Christians in the world of business are likely to meet. This is an excellent example of the way the moral-cultural system shapes the attitudes and behavior of those within an economic system. It vivifies, directs, and restrains the latter not by subordinating it institutionally but by supplying it with a way of life that gives it spirit.

Williams and Houck's cases open up another category of moral problem as well—the problem of a democratic capitalist system in

---

[71] Oliver F. Williams and John W. Houck, *Full Value: Cases in Christian Business Ethics* (New York: Harper & Row, 1978), p. xv.

interaction with an entire world of other cultures and other economic and political systems. They mention, for example, the problems of Gulf & Western in the Dominican Republic, an American hotel chain in Jamaica, a resolution of the U.S. Senate on world hunger, and a corporation with branches in South Africa. In these cases the authors raise important issues, though they are perhaps a little less critical of conventional pieties on these issues than on others and a little one-sided in their conception of the empirical situation.

From the theology of economics sketched above and even more from the notes offered toward a theology of democratic capitalism, it follows that U.S. business enterprises abroad represent not simply an economic system alone but also a political and a moral-cultural system. They are, willy-nilly, agents of democratic capitalism, not of free enterprise alone. Moreover, unless they succeed in establishing on foreign soil at least some of the political culture and some of the moral culture in which alone democratic capitalism can be incarnated, they are doomed to lose spiritual legitimacy. Without the latter, freely bestowed, they are bound to be regarded as illegitimate enterprises. In the long run—and, often enough, even in the short run of five or ten years—such moral status is bound to have damaging consequences for the business enterprises themselves and for the political and moral-cultural systems they represent. On the one hand, impossible political and cultural burdens cannot be imposed on business enterprises. They have not been constituted as primary agents of the political or moral-cultural system, and asking them to do well what they are not set up to do is asking too much. On the other hand, they cannot escape the burden of carrying with them the presuppositions of their own native political and moral-cultural systems. To these, too, they must do at least rough justice.

Direct political interference on the part of American enterprises abroad would be fiercely, and properly, resisted. So would a sort of tacit moral-cultural imperialism. Yet the international war of ideas cannot be evaded. Cultures that are not democratic capitalist do not observe the differentiation between an economic system, a political system, and a moral system. Both traditional authoritarian and social-ist regimes have unitary theories and practices of control, and both attack the differentiation required by democratic capitalism. Corpo-rations must become far more intellectually aware of the maelstrom of ideas, beliefs, and practices they enter.

In this respect the debate about the social responsibility of busi-ness has been badly drawn. Though not designed to be either political institutions or moral-cultural institutions, business enterprises are, as it were, plants that cannot flourish independently of the trebly differentiated roots from which they have sprung. Their responsibility to themselves entails sophisticated attention to the political and moral-cultural requirements of their own existence. Such are the fact of life of democratic capitalism.

The most urgent question posed by Williams and Houck concerns world poverty and hunger. They borrow from Father Hesburgh's *The Humane Imperative*[72] the image of a spaceship containing five spacemen, one of whom (representing the populations of the democratic capitalist lands) produces and uses 80 percent of the spacecraft's goods. Two centuries ago, the United States and Western Europe were not democratic-capitalist lands, nor had they escaped from poverty. They were state-controlled mercantilist societies with widespread poverty, recurrent famine, and "underdeveloped" transport, living conditions, and diet. These nations, like others, were threatened by the Malthusian trap. How did they escape the poverty, disease, ignorance, and material precariousness they then shared with most of the rest of the world?

They did it by following an idea. Many scoffed at the idea; many rejected it. It is a dynamic idea, not complete once and for all time. It is experimental in temper. It is rooted in the differentiation of the economic, the political, and the moral-cultural systems. It interprets human society as so composed by the Creator that its greatest source of social dynamism is the imagination, initiative, and liberty of the human individual. It is an idea whose express purpose is to increase the material wealth of all nations, at the very least eliminating famine and poverty.

There are today no democratic-capitalist nations that cannot feed themselves. Major socialist nations, which used to be net exporters of food, are no longer able to feed themselves.[73] Many traditional societies, down through history subject to famine, still endure it. None of this hunger is necessary, for it is not caused by ignorance about agriculture. Its sources are preeminently to be found in economic and political institutions that needlessly stifle elementary economic growth.

[72] Theodore M. Hesburgh, *The Humane Imperative: A Challenge for the Year 2000* (New Haven, Conn.: Yale University Press, 1974), p. 101, quoted in Williams and Houck, *Full Value*, p. 135.

[73] Ideological blinders cause much needless suffering. Soviet planners know what works but cannot admit it. "By law, no Soviet citizen can farm a private plot larger than 1 acre. Nevertheless, private farmers working 1.4% of the country's arable land produce 61% of its potatoes, 34% of the eggs and 29% of the meat, milk and vegetable output." *Newsweek*, April 7, 1980, p. 21.

No person of conscience can remain indifferent to hunger and poverty. The great intellectual and moral argument of our time is not whether we should do all we can to raise the material wealth of all nations but what we ought to do and how. The greatest irresponsibility of all would be to pretend we know nothing about how to produce wealth, or that the knowledge was not implanted on this earth by the Maker of all things, so that His creatures, by trial and error, would in due course discover it.

It is the ethical responsibility of Christians who enter the business corporation to recognize that their way of life has a twofold importance for the entire world: the spiritual importance of a set of ideas and the material importance of showing all nations a way out of famine and misery. Now that the secrets of how to produce wealth are known, famine and misery spring not from the will of God but from the will of man.

# 2

# Toward a Theology
# of the Corporation

Our task is to set forth some steps toward a theology of the corporation. We need such a theology so that the ministers who serve businessmen and workers might be able to preach more illuminating and practical sermons and so that critics might have at their disposal a theologically sound standard of behavior for corporations.

For many years one of my favorite texts in scripture has been Isaiah 53:2–3: "He hath no form nor comeliness; and when we shall see him, there is no beauty that we should desire him. He is despised and rejected of men; a man of sorrows, and acquainted with grief; he was despised, and we esteemed him not." I would like to apply these words to the modern business corporation, a much despised incarnation of God's presence in this world.

When we speak of the body of Christ, we ordinarily mean the church, both invisible and visible, both sinless and marred by sin. God calls His followers to bring His presence to their work, to their daily milieu, to history. This is the doctrine of Christian vocation. A liturgy does not end without a word of mission: "Go out into the world of daily work to carry the peace and love of Jesus Christ." I do not mean by this to suggest that the Christian form is the only form of speech for this fundamental attitude. A sense of vocation infuses Jews, Muslims, and others of religious faith. Many who are not religious also regard their work as useful and ennobling. They feel called to the task of making life better for their fellow human beings. But I am a Catholic Christian, and it is better to speak in the idiom with most meaning for me than to pretend to an idiom that, by virtue of being no more than a common denominator, would appear superficial to all of us.

To work in a modern business corporation, no one need pass a test of faith or even reveal his or her religious convictions to others.

But it would be a mistake to permit the business corporation's commendable acceptance of religious pluralism to mask the religious vocation that many see in it.

## The Multinational Corporation

In speaking of the corporation, I will concentrate on those large business corporations that are found among the 300 or so multinational corporations, two-thirds of which are American.[1]

The reason one must first consider these *big* corporations is that all but very strict socialists seem to be in favor of markets, ownership, cooperatives, and *small* business. Religious socialists like John C. Cort favor the private ownership of small businesses, ownership through cooperatives, and some free-market mechanisms.[2]

What are multinational corporations? They are not those which merely sell their goods in other lands, buy goods from other lands, or trade with other lands. Multinationals are corporations that build manufacturing or other facilities in other lands in order to operate there. The building of a base of operations in other lands is an important condition for qualification as a multinational corporation in the strict sense. One should not think only of factories; banks and insurance firms—important for local investment—may also establish such operations.

The training of an indigenous labor and managerial force is not a strictly necessary condition for a corporation to be considered multinational, but it is a common characteristic, particularly of American companies. Thus multinationals make four chief contributions to the host country. Of these the first two, (1) capital facilities and (2) technological transfers inherent in the training of personnel, remain forever in the host country, whatever the ultimate fate of the original company. In addition, products manufactured within the nation no longer have to be imported; thus (3) the host nation's problems with balance of payments are eased. Finally, (4) wages paid to employees remain in the country, and local citizens begin to invest in the corporation, so that most of its future capital can be generated locally.[3] These are important factors in any accounting of the relative

[1] Sperry Lea and Simon Webley, *Multinational Corporations in Developed Countries: A Review of Recent Research and Policy Thinking* (Washington, D.C.: British-North American Committee, 1973), p. 1.

[2] See John C. Cort, "Can Socialism Be Distinguished from Marxism?" *Cross Currents* 29 (Winter 1979-1980): 423-34.

[3] Ronald E. Muller estimates that 80 percent of the capital raised by multinational corporations in Latin America is local: "We find initially that, for the period

wealth transferred to and from the host country and the country of the corporation's origin. Critics sometimes concentrate only on the flow of return on investment. They commonly neglect to add up the capital investment, training, balance-of-payments relief, salaries, and stimulation of local investment.

Almost all of the 200 American multinationals are to be found among *Fortune*'s 500 industrial companies, though a few are among the largest banks and insurance firms. What less-developed countries want most today is manufactured goods, at prices made possible by local production, and the financial services of banks and insurance companies.

Generally speaking, only a company of the size represented by the *Fortune* 500 has the capital and skills to accept the risks of operating in an unfamiliar culture. As it is, 40 percent of all foreign sales of U.S. multinationals are in Western Europe, and another 25 percent are in Japan, Canada, Taiwan, Hong Kong, South Korea, Australia, and other industrial nations. Most concerns about the multinationals, however, focus on their role in the developing nations. Only about 12 percent of the business of U.S. multinationals is to be found in Latin America, and only a tiny fraction in Africa. Vast expanses of the whole world never see an American multinational.[4]

The vast majority of U.S. corporations are not multinationals. Many that could be do not wish to be, believing the headaches more costly than the rewards. Some that are multinationals refuse to build operations under unstable conditions, such as those characterizing most of the developing nations. That is why such a small proportion of overseas activity by U.S. multinationals is to be found in Latin America and Africa.

Other contextual matters should be noted. In most nations of the world—notably the socialist nations—private corporations are not permitted to come into existence. Only a few nations of the world produce privately held corporations. Furthermore, some nations which do so (like the United States) were formerly colonies, and some others (Hong Kong) still are. Since economic development depends to a

from 1957 to 1965, of the total U.S. investment in Latin America only 17 per cent of the actual financial capital investments ever came from the United States. When we look at the manufacturing sector for the same period, we find that 78 per cent of all U.S. corporate investments were financed not from U.S. savings but from Latin American savings." "The Multinational Corporation: Asset or Impediment to World Justice?" in *Poverty, Environment and Power*, ed. Paul Hallock (New York: International Documentation on the Contemporary Church— North America, 1973), p. 42.

[4] U.S. Bureau of the Census, *Statistical Abstract of the United States, 1979*, (Washington, D.C.: U.S. Department of Commerce, 1979), table 944.

large extent upon home-based privately held corporations, differences in moral-cultural climate are significant. Some cultures seem to develop far higher proportions of skilled inventors, builders, and managers of industry than others do. In some cultures, the work force is more productive than in others.

Over time, education and training may provide new moral models and fairly swift cultural development. Simultaneously, of course, such developments may provoke intense conflicts with guardians of the earlier cultural order. It cannot be stressed too often that corporations are not merely economic agencies. They are also moral-cultural agencies. They may come into existence, survive, and prosper only under certain moral-cultural conditions.

It goes without saying that private corporations depend upon a nonsocialist, nonstatist political order. Insofar as socialist governments in Yugoslavia and elsewhere are now experimenting with autonomous economic enterprises, taking their signals from a free market, and rewarding their managers and workers according to profit and loss, they are moving toward a democratic capitalist political order. As their middle class grows, so will the demand for further political rights, due process, democratic methods, a free press, freedom of worship, and the rest. Economic liberties require political liberties, and vice versa. Historically, not only has private business enterprise grown up with liberal democracy, it has also been the main engine in destroying class distinctions between aristocrats and serfs, by making possible personal and social mobility on a massive scale.

The private business corporation is particularly active among Americans. As Oscar Handlin has pointed out, the United States in 1800, with a population of just over 4 million, already had more corporations than all the nations of Europe combined.[5] Some of these corporations began to grow into large-scale organizations—roughly, following the railroads—at the end of the nineteenth century.

Nearly all American corporations, and particularly those in the *Fortune* 500, originated around a novel invention. They grew in sales, size, and capital either through products never before known or through novel processes for producing them. Entire industries, like those for airplanes, automobiles, oil, gas, electricity, television, cinema, computers, copiers, office machinery, electronics, and plastics, are based on corporations initially formed by the American inventors of their products.

---

[5] Oscar Handlin, "The Development of the Corporation," in *The Corporation: A Theological Inquiry*, ed. Michael Novak and John W. Cooper (Washington, D.C.: American Enterprise Institute, 1981).

## Theological Beginnings

In thinking about the corporation in history and its theological significance, I begin with a general theological principle. George Bernanos
once said that grace is everywhere. Wherever we look in the world,
there are signs of God's presence: in the mountains, in a grain of sand,
in a human person, in the poor and the hungry. The earth is charged
with the grandeur of God. So is human history.

If we look for signs of grace in the corporation, we may discern
seven of them—a suitably sacramental number.

**Creativity.** The Creator locked great riches in nature, riches to be
discovered only gradually through human effort. John Locke observed
that the yield of the most favored field in Britain could be increased
a hundredfold if human ingenuity and human agricultural science
were applied to its productivity.[6] Nature alone is not as fecund as
nature under intelligent cultivation. The world, then, is immeasurably
rich as it comes from the Creator, but only potentially so. This potential was hidden for thousands of years until human discovery
began to release portions of it for human benefit. Yet even today
we have not yet begun to imagine all the possibilities of wealth in the
world the Creator designed. The limits of our present intelligence
restrict the human race to the relative poverty in which it still lives.

In 1979 Atlantic Richfield ran an advertisement based on a theme
first enunciated, as far as I can tell, by Father Hesburgh of Notre
Dame, namely, that 40 percent of the world's energy is used by the
6 percent of the world's population residing in the United States.[7]
This way of putting the facts is an example of the cultivation of guilt
that Professor Bauer has described.[8] A moment's thought shows that
it is a preposterous formulation.

What the entire human race meant by energy until the discovery
of the United States and the inventions promoted by its political
economy were the natural forces of sun, wind, moving water, animals,
and human muscle. Thomas Aquinas traveled on foot or by burro
from Rome to Paris and back seven times in his life. The first pope
to be able to make that voyage by train did so six centuries later, in
the mid-nineteenth century. Until then, people traveled exactly as

[6] John Locke, *Second Treatise of Civil Government* (New York: Macmillan Co.,
1947), p. 20.
[7] Theodore Hesburgh, *The Humane Imperative: A Challenge for the Year 2000*
(New Haven, Conn.: Yale University Press, 1974), p. 101.
[8] P. T. Bauer, "Western Guilt and Third World Poverty," in *Corporation*, ed.
Novak and Cooper.

they had done since the time of Christ and before—by horse and carriage, by donkey, or by foot. History for a very long time seemed relatively static. The social order did not promote inventions and new technologies, at least to the degree lately reached. The method of scientific discovery had not been invented.

In 1809 an American outside Philadelphia figured out how to ignite anthracite coal. The ability to use anthracite, which burned hotter and more steadily than bituminous coal, made practical the seagoing steamship and the locomotive.

In 1859 the first oil well was dug outside of Titusville, Pennsylvania. Oil was known in biblical times but used only for products like perfume and ink. Arabia would have been as rich then as now, if anybody had known what to do with the black stuff.

The invention of the piston engine and the discovery of how to drill for oil were also achieved in the United States. The first electric light bulb was illuminated in 1879 in Edison, New Jersey.

After World War II the U.S. government dragooned the utilities into experimenting with nuclear energy. They knew nothing about it. They did not need it. They did not want it. Oil and coal were cheap. The government, however, promoted the peaceful uses of the atom.

Thus 100 percent of what the modern world means by energy was invented by 6 percent of the world's population. More than 60 percent of that energy had been distributed to the rest of the world. Though the United States can, of course, do better than that, we need not feel guilty for inventing forms of energy as useful to the human race as the fire brought to earth by Prometheus.

The agency through which inventions and discoveries are made productive for the human race is the corporation. Its creativity makes available to mass markets the riches long hidden in Creation. Its creativity mirrors God's. That is the standard by which its deeds and misdeeds are properly judged.

**Liberty.** The corporation mirrors God's presence also in its liberty, by which I mean independence from the state. That independence was the greatest achievement of the much-despised but creative 6 percent of the world's population. Advancing the work of their forebears, they invented the concept and framed the laws that for the first time in history set boundaries on the state, ruling certain activities off-limits to its interference. Rights of person and home, free speech in public, a free press, and other liberties came to be protected both by constitutional law and by powerful interests actively empowered to defend themselves under that law. Legal autonomy was such that even the king could not forcibly enter the home of a peasant; a peasant's home was as protected as a duke's castle—rights which the colonists in America demanded for themselves. Private business corporations were permitted to become agents of experimentation, of trial and error, and for good reason: to unleash economic activism. The state retained rights and obligations of regulation, and undertook the indirect promotion of industry and commerce. The state alone was prohibited from becoming the sole economic agent. A sphere of economic liberty was created.

The purpose of this liberty was to unlock greater riches than the world had ever known. Liberty was to be an experiment, which Adam Smith and others advocated, that might (or might not) prove to be in accordance with nature and with the laws of human society. Pleading for room to experiment, their practical, empirical arguments flew in the face of entrenched ideological opposition. The case for liberty prevailed.

The foundational concept of democratic capitalism, then, is not, as Marx thought, private property. It is limited government. Private property, of course, is one limitation on government.[9] What is interesting about private property is not that *I* own something, that *I* possess; its heart is not "possessive individualism," in C. B. MacPherson's phrase.[10] Quite the opposite. The key is that the state is limited by being forbidden to control all rights and all goods. It cannot infringe on the privacy of one's home or on one's right to the fruit of one's labors and risks. Herbert Stein has a useful definition of capitalism: "The idea of a capitalist system has nothing to do with capital and has everything to do with freedom. I think of capitalism as a system in which ability to obtain and use income independently of other persons or organizations, including government, is widely distributed among the individuals of the population." [11]

This is the distinctively American way of thinking about private property. In this framework, property is important less for its material reality than for the legal rights its ownership and use represent and for the limits it imposes on the power of the state. Such liberty was indispensable if private business corporations were to come into existence. Such corporations give liberty economic substance over and against the state.

9 See Paul Johnson, "Is There a Moral Basis for Capitalism?" in *Democracy and Mediating Structures: A Theological Inquiry*, ed. Michael Novak (Washington, D.C.: American Enterprise Institute, 1980), pp. 49-58.
10 C. B. MacPherson, *The Political Theory of Possessive Individualism: Hobbes to Locke* (New York: Oxford University Press, 1962), p. 263.
11 Herbert Stein, *Capitalism—If You Can Keep It* (Washington, D.C.: American Enterprise Institute, 1980), p. 6.

**Birth and Mortality.** In coming into being with a technological break-through, and then perishing when some new technology causes it to be replaced, a typical corporation mirrors the cycle of birth and mortality. New corporations arise every day; dead ones litter history. Examining the *Fortune* 500 at ten-year intervals shows that even large corporations are subject to the cycle: New ones keep appearing, and many that were once prominent disappear. Of the original *Fortune* 500, first listed in 1954, only 285 remained in 1974. Of the missing 215, 159 had merged, 50 had become too small or gone out of business, and 6 were reclassified or had unavailable data.[12] Recently, Chrysler has been number 10. Will it by 1990 be gone from the list? Will Ford be gone from the list? It is entirely possible. As products of human liberty, corporations rise and fall, live and die. One does not have in them a lasting home—or even an immortal enemy.

**Social Motive.** Corporations, as the very word suggests, are not individualistic in their conception, in their operations, or in their purposes. Adam Smith entitled his book *An Inquiry into the Nature and Causes of the Wealth of Nations*. Its social scope went beyond individuals and beyond Great Britain to include all nations. The fundamental intention of the system from the beginning has been the wealth of all humanity.

The invention of democratic capitalism, the invention of the corporation, and the liberation of the corporations from total control by state bureaucracies (although some control always, and properly, remains) were intended to be multinational. Smith foresaw an interdependent world, for the first time able to overcome immemorial famine, poverty, and misery. He imagined people of every race, every culture, and every religion adopting the new knowledge about the causes of wealth. One does not need to be Christian or Jewish, or to share the Judeo-Christian world view, to understand the religious and economic potency of the free economy. Smith did not exactly foresee Toyota and Sony. But he certainly would have been delighted to add a chapter to his immense study showing how the Japanese demonstrated the truth of his hypothesis.[13]

**Social Character.** The corporation is inherently and in its essence corporate. The very word suggests communal, nonindividual, many acting together. Those who describe capitalism by stressing the indi-

---

12 "The 500: A Report on Two Decades," *Fortune*, May 1975, p. 238.

13 Per capita savings deposits in Japan at the end of 1977 were $9,531, compared with $4,354 in the United States. See *Facts and Figures of Japan* (Tokyo: Tokyo Foreign Press Center, 1980).

vidual entrepreneur miss the central point. Buying and selling by individual entrepreneurs occurred in biblical times. What is interesting and novel—at least what struck Max Weber as interesting and novel—is the communal focus of the new ethos: the rise of communal risk taking, the pooling of resources, the sense of communal religious vocation in economic activism. To be sure, certain developments in law and in techniques of accounting had to occur before corporations could be institutionalized in their modern form. In this sense, too, they are social creations.

Corporations depend on the emergence of an infrastructure in intellectual life that makes possible new forms of communal collaboration. They depend on ideas that are powerful and clear enough to organize thousands of persons around common tasks. Moreover, these ideas must be strong enough to endure for years, so that individuals who commit themselves to them can expect to spend thirty to forty years working out their vocation. For many millions of religious persons the daily milieu in which they work out their salvation is the communal, corporate world of the workplace. For many, the workplace is a kind of second family. Even those who hate their work often like their co-workers. This is often true in factories; it is also true in offices. Comradeship is natural to humans. Labor unions properly build on it.

**Insight.** The primary capital of any corporation is insight, invention, finding a better way. Insight is of many kinds and plays many roles: it is central to invention; it lies at the heart of organization; it is the vital force in strategies for innovation, production, and marketing. Corporate management works hard at communal insight. Constantly, teams of persons meet to brainstorm and work out common strategies. Insight is the chief resource of any corporation, and there cannot be too much of it. Its scarcity is called stupidity.

Karl Marx erred in thinking that capital has to do primarily with machinery, money, and other tangible instruments of production. He overlooked the extent to which the primary form of capital is an idea.[14]

---

[14] "Economy is essentially the transformation of natural forces and natural goods into forces and goods that serve humanity. It is an order created by thinking people, and one that has developed as a result of people's intellectual and spiritual growth. Further, it should be clear that when we regard economy as the creation of thinking human beings, economic wealth becomes nothing more than the transformation of natural wealth. There is no material wealth except that of nature and that created by humans from nature." Stephen B. Roman and Eugen Loebl, *The Responsible Society* (New York: Regina Ryan Books/Two Continents, 1977), pp. 22-23.

The right to patent industrial ideas is an extremely important constitutional liberty. It is indispensable to the life of corporations, as indispensable as the copyright is to writers. Money without ideas is not yet capital. Machinery is only as good as the idea it embodies. The very word "capital," from the Latin *caput*, "head," points to the human spirit as the primary form of wealth. The miser sitting on his gold is not a capitalist. The investor with an idea is a capitalist. Insight makes the difference.

A momentary digression. Money was more material before capitalism, when it was gold and silver coin, than it came to be afterward. Under capitalism, perhaps a majority of transactions are intellectualized "book" transactions. Moreover, paper money is necessary, as are stocks, bonds, constitutions, and legal contracts. Materialism is more and more left behind as money depends for its value less on material substance than on public confidence, the health of the social order, the stability of institutions. Let these be threatened and investments flee because deteriorating social health reduces the value of the amounts registered on paper. Materially, money is often "not worth the paper it's printed on." Its real value depends on sociality, trust, a sense of health and permanence. In this respect, a theological treatise on the symbolic nature of money is badly needed. Such a treatise would have to deal not only with the fact that most money exists only in the intellectual realm but also with the impersonality of money, which transcends discrimination based on race, religion, sex, or nationality, and with money's remarkable indeterminacy, according to which its moral value springs from how persons, in their liberty, use it. Money opens a vast range of freedom of choice. Accordingly, it is more closely related to insight and liberty than to matter. It no longer functions as it did in biblical times.

**The Rise of Liberty and Election.** A corporation risks liberty and election; it is part of its romance to do so. Tremendous mistakes in strategy can cripple even the largest companies. Easy Washing Machines of Syracuse once made an excellent washing machine, but Maytag's discovery of a new technology took away part of Easy's market. Easy had all its assets sunk in a plant that it could not redesign quickly enough to incorporate the new technology, and the company collapsed. Thus a sudden technological breakthrough, even a relatively minor one, can cripple a company or an industry. A simple strategic mistake by a team of corporate executives about where to apply the company's energies over a year or two can end up dimming the company's outlook for many years. A failure to modernize can bring about bankruptcy. The corporation operates in a world of no scientific certainty, in which corporate leaders must constantly make judgments about reality when not all the evidence about reality is in. Such leaders argue among themselves about strategic alternatives, each perhaps saying to himself, "We will see who is right about this," or "The next year or two will tell." But a judgment must be made and the investment committed before the telling is completed. Thus decision makers often experience the risks inherent in their decisions. At the very least they always face the risk of doing considerably less well than they think they are going to do.

In these seven ways, corporations offer metaphors for grace, a kind of insight into God's ways in history. Yet corporations are of this world. They sin. They are *semper reformanda*—always in need of reform.

## Problems of Bigness and Other Accusations

Big corporations are despised and rejected even when the market system, small businesses, and private ownership are not. Some religious socialists do not absolutely reject certain elements in the democratic-capitalist idea. But they often bridle at the big corporations. Their accusations against such corporations—many of them as true as charges made against the universities or against any large institution—are many.

One accusation is that the corporations are autocratic, that internally they are not democratic. In trying to decide how true this charge is, one could undertake a survey of the management techniques of the *Fortune* 500 corporations. How are they actually managed? How does their management differ in practice from the internal management of universities, churches, government agencies, or other institutions? Let us suppose that some autocrats still function in various spheres of authority today, including business. What sanctions are available to autocrats within a corporation? Leadership in all spheres today seems to depend upon large areas of consensus; leaders seem to "manage" more than they "command." I have roughly the same impression of the chief executive officers I have met as of the American Catholic bishops I have met; namely, that out of the office they would find it hard, as Schumpeter says, to say boo to a duck. Few, as I see them, are autocrats. Would that the world still saw the likes of Cardinals Spellman, Connell, Cushing, and Gibbons; or of industrial autocrats like Carnegie, Mellon, and others. Such types seem to have perished from the earth. In their place are men who, if you saw them in sport shirts at a Ramada Inn, would make you think you had dropped in on a convention of real-estate agents from Iowa. Very pleasant, nice men, they are nowhere near as assertive as journalists. They do not often have the occupational arrogance of academics. But empirical tests are in order to see how many autocrats are in corporations, in comparison with any other sphere of life.

A second frequent accusation against big corporations is the alienation their employees experience in the workplace. To what extent is such alienation caused by the conditions of modern work under any existing system or under any imaginable system? Do laborers in auto factories in Bratislava or Poznán work under conditions any different from those faced by laborers in the United States? One ought to compare hours of work, conditions of the workplace, salaries, working procedures, and levels of pollution. There is no evidence that any real or imagined socialism can take the modernity out of modern work. Nor is boring work unique to the modern factory; it surely dominated the ancient work of European peasants and continues to dominate the fourteen-hour day of the modern potato farmer. Farming is not, in my experience, inherently less alienating than working seven hours, with time off for lunch, on an assembly line.

Alienation is not a problem peculiar to capitalism or to corporations. Is work less alienating within a government bureaucracy? Instead of condemning political activists or politicians to jail for various crimes, suppose one simply condemned them to filing the correspondence of congressmen from states like Ohio and Arkansas for periods of up to three months.

A third accusation against corporations is that they represent too great a concentration of power. What is the alternative? There is indeed a circle within which small is beautiful, a relatively small and beautiful circle. But "small is beautiful" does not apply across the whole large world. When Jane Fonda and Tom Hayden made their pilgrimage to seventy-two cities carrying the word on economic democracy, they did not fly in airplanes made in mom and pop stores. Their travel arrangements were made not by small organizations working off a telephone in a back room, but by agencies with computers and Telex connections to operating stations in all airlines and in all airports, giving them the instantaneous information required to synchronize such a trip in a very short time.

Socialist economist Robert Lekachman has argued that the big corporations should be reduced in size to more manageable proportions.[15] Maybe so. To my mind the question is a practical, experi-

15 "A second characteristic I would seek from socialism is a reduction in the scale of the corporation in our country. Now, this is not 'small is beautiful.' I do not think you are going to build large aircraft with E. F. Schumacher's intermediate technology—nor, for that matter, large computers in local workshops.

mental one. Consider the largest of all corporations, General Motors. It is already broken up into more than 200 units in more than 177 congressional districts in the United States. Its largest single facility, in Michigan, employs no more than 14,000 people. Many universities—the University of Michigan and Michigan State, to name two—comprise human communities two or three times that size. Corporations already follow the principle of subsidiarity far more thoroughly than Lekachman seems to take into account. One might argue that they should be still smaller. Yet one must note that the smaller U.S. auto companies—American Motors, Chrysler, and Ford—are apparently in danger of perishing because of inadequate capital to meet the enormous expenses of retooling for new auto technologies. The foreign auto companies competing with General Motors (even in the United States) are also very large. If small is beautiful, its beauty seems precarious indeed; big may be necessary.

In practice, I cannot imagine how human capacities and human choices of the sort needed by mass markets could still be made available except through large organizations. Small organizations may suit a small country, but it seems to me absurd to imagine that a continental nation with a population of 220 million can be well served in all respects only through small organizations in small industries. If somebody can invent a system of smallness, fine; I am not, in principle, against it. I just cannot imagine that it can work in practice.

Corporations are further accused of being inherently evil because they work for a profit. Without profit no new capital is made available for research, development, and new investment. Further, there is a difference between maximization of profit and optimization of profit. To aim at maximizing profit—that is, to obtain the greatest profit possible out of every opportunity—is to be greedy in the present at the expense of the future. The profit maximizer demands too much for products that can be produced more cheaply by somebody else and in the process narrows his market and destroys his reputation. Inevitably, he damages himself and, in time, destroys himself. Adam Smith made this point a long time ago, and history is replete with

---

Nevertheless, by every account, the scale of the large corporation is much less related to technological economies of scale than to various advertising, marketing, financial, and legal benefits—including the opportunity to control markets.

"Now, free enterprise economists, of course, would be alarmed by the idea of limiting the size of corporations. I would argue that competition only works where it exists; and the scale of the large organization frequently limits the amount of effective competition that can occur. Diminishing the average size of the productive units would increase their number, and thereby the potential for competition." Robert Lekachman, "The Promise of Democratic Socialism," in *Democracy and Mediating Structures*, ed. Novak, p. 40.

examples of it. By contrast, to optimize profit is to take many other factors besides profit into account, including long-term new investment, consumer loyalty, and the sense of a fair service for a fair price.

The profit motive must necessarily operate in a socialist economy, too. Every economy that intends to progress must have as its motive the ability to get more out of the economic process than it puts in. Unless there is a return on investment, the economy simply spins its wheels in stagnation, neither accumulating nor growing. Capital accumulation is what profits are called in socialist enterprises. If the Soviets invest money in dams or in building locomotives, they must get back at least what they invest or they lose money. If they do lose money—and they often do—then they must draw on other resources. And if they do that throughout the system, economic stagnation and decline are inevitable. The same law binds both socialist and capitalist economies: Economic progress, growth, and forward motion cannot occur unless the return on investment is larger than the investment itself.

It is true that under socialism profits belong to the state and are allocated to individuals by the state for the state's own purposes. Such a procedure can be institutionalized, but the costs of enforcing it are great. It tremendously affects the possibilities of liberty, of choice. It deeply affects incentives and creativity.

Objections to corporations are many. Some are clearly justified. Some are spurious. A full-dress theology of the corporation would properly evaluate each one fairly, from many points of view. A convenient summary of some of them is to be found in *The Crisis of the Corporation*, by Richard J. Barnet.[16] Barnet makes three major accusations: (1) that the multinational corporations have inordinate power; (2) that they weaken the powers of the nation-state; and (3) that their actual practice destroys several "myths" about corporations.

The power of the multinational corporations, Barnet believes, springs from their ability to internationalize planning, production, finance, and marketing. In planning, each part can specialize, so that the whole pursues "profit maximization." In production, resources from various lands are integrated. In finance, computerization allows multinational corporations to take advantage of fluctuations in capital markets. In marketing, goods and consumption are standardized.[17]

From another point of view, these accusations seem to list *advantages*. Any economic organization which can work as Barnet describes would seem to be well placed to produce the maximum number of

[16] Richard J. Barnet, *The Crisis of the Corporation* (Washington, D.C.: Institute for Policy Studies, 1975).
[17] Ibid., pp. 7-8.

goods at the lowest cost. This efficiency should have the effect of making the most practical use of scarce capital, while increasing that capital through profitable investment. (We have already noted an important difference between "profit maximization" and "profit optimization.") The purpose of an interdependent world economic order is to match off the strengths of one region with those of another: a region with capital reserves and high labor costs is needed by a region without capital reserves but cheap labor. The cost of ignoring each other would be high for both regions. Cooperation should produce benefits for both.

Barnet argues that the powers of nation-states are weakened because multinational corporations make intracorporate transfers of funds without the knowledge of national governmental bodies. In addition, he asserts, they shift production to low-wage areas with fewer "union troubles"; move productive facilities to regions where tax advantages are greatest; have no loyalty to any one country; and use dominance in one national market to achieve dominance in others because they can "out-advertise" smaller local companies.[18]

If all of these assertions are true, at least sometimes and in some places, not all of their effects are evil. Consider, for example, the competition between Japanese, European, and U.S. automobile manufacturers. The new reality is that market competition has been internationalized. Every such new development has advantages and costs. It appears that U.S. citizens benefit by quality and cost from this competition. Obviously, foreign auto workers would seem to benefit. Unless U.S. manufacturers can do better, U.S. auto workers will continue to suffer.

Would the world be a better place if each nation-state tried solely to protect its own industries? At various times, protectionism has triumphed. Nations do have the power to expel, close out, restrict, and nationalize foreign industries; often they do. This course, too, has costs as well as advantages. Barnet does not show that its costs are lower than those of the competition he opposes. No matter how Chrysler advertised during 1979, it did not seem to move the cars it tried to sell. Advertising is far less exact than he imagines.

Barnet argues, finally, that monopolization undercuts competitive free enterprise. He concedes that monopoly scarcely exists, but hastens to substitute for it oligopoly (four major firms, for example, controlling a majority of sales in several industries), whose "effects are much the same." [19] He argues that efficiency is undercut by intra-

18 Ibid., pp. 8-11.
19 Ibid., p. 14.

corporate transactions (as when tax laws encourage the shipment of products over long distances, when similar products could be acquired locally);[20] that income distribution between the top 20 percent and the bottom 20 percent of income earners in the United States has "remained the same for forty-five years";[21] and that democracy is not enhanced by a free economy.[22]

Since Barnet himself is in favor of state monopolies in the socialist pattern, his objections to "oligopolies" do not have an authentic ring. Surely, four large companies in an industry are better than one state monopoly. Moreover, in the international field, the three major U.S. automobile companies, for example, compete not only with each other but also with Volvo, Fiat, Peugeot, Volkswagen, Toyota, and many others. In other industries, international competition is also a reality.[23]

It is true that prices in a complex, highly technological industry are not a simple matter, but it goes too far to suggest that they are no longer a useful indicator of cost and value. Consumers today make economic choices not only between cars to buy but between buying a car and investing the money, or building an addition on the house, or doing something else. In seeking the consumers' dollars, producers compete not only with others in their own industries but also with other industries altogether. Pricing, however sophisticated the process through which prices are calculated, still affects the decisions of purchasers, as alternative marketing strategies amply demonstrate.

With respect to income distribution, most socialists today recognize that incomes are not and cannot be perfectly equal. They certainly are not in socialist countries. If persons at the top end of the income ladder receive eight times as much as those at the bottom, it follows that the total share of income of those at the top will be significantly higher than that of a similar cohort at the bottom. This relationship is strictly arithmetical. Imagine that Barnet himself earns $50,000 a year from his salary and royalties. This income would rank in the top 3 percent of all U.S. households, seven times as high as the official poverty level for a nonfarm family of four.[24]

[20] Ibid., pp. 16-17.

[21] Ibid., p. 20.

[22] Ibid., pp. 21-22.

[23] Lester Thurow, "Let's Abolish the Antitrust Laws," *The New York Times*, October 19, 1980.

[24] "The poverty threshold for a non-farm family of four was $7,412 in 1979." U.S. Bureau of the Census, *Money Income and Poverty Status of Families and Persons in the United States: 1979 (Advanced Report)* (Washington, D.C., 1970), p. 1.

Arithmetically, his class—say, that of the top 5 percent—must accumulate a disproportionate share of all U.S. incomes.

There is a further point. One must not compare only percentiles—snapshots of groups at one point in time. As a graduate student at Harvard Law School, Barnet's income was certainly lower than it is now; it may even have been below the poverty level (though this did not, except technically, make him "poor"). At each decade thereafter one would expect his income to place him in a different percentile. While percentiles may remain relatively constant, individuals (at least in a free, mobile society) rise and fall between them. Moreover, a family's relative wealth in the long run—over, say, three generations—depends largely on the sort of investment it makes with available funds. Investments in consumption at each moment preclude growth; investment in education, property, and the like make future material improvement probable. Thus, in many families, one generation works not solely for itself but for its future progeny. As it happens, families once wealthy sometimes experience economic decline, and families once poor sometimes become better off than in earlier generations. One must track not simply the statistical percentiles but the rise and fall over time of individuals and families within these percentiles. One would expect some individuals and families to be more intelligent, wiser, and luckier over time than others. Inequality of income is no more a scandal than are inequalities of looks, personality, talent, will, and luck. Inequality of income appears to be an inevitable fact in all large societies.

There is a peculiar historical link—which even Marxists recognize—between the emergence of liberal democracy in Great Britain, the United States, the Netherlands, and a few cognate lands and the emergence of a free economy. One might be satisfied to stress the historical character of the link. But it also seems to have a necessary conceptual character as well. If individuals lack fundamental economic liberties (to earn, spend, save, and invest as they see fit), they necessarily have few effective political liberties. If they are dependent upon the state for economic decisions, they must be wards of the state in other matters. Moreover, to believe that state bureaucrats are competent to make economic decisions for the common good is to make a great leap of faith, when one considers the actual economic well-being of workers in the U.S.S.R., Poland, Cuba, Yugoslavia. Even the democratic socialists of Sweden and West Germany insist upon vital economic liberties for individuals and corporations.

Socialist societies do not permit private corporations to exist. They operate on the assumption that state officials know best what is for the common good. In reflecting on their actual practice, one may come to believe that democratic capitalism is more likely to meet the goals of socialism—plus other goals of its own—than socialism is. The social instrument invented by democratic capitalism to achieve social goals is the private corporation. Anyone can start one; those who succeed in making them work add to the common benefit. Yet corporations do not live (or die) in a vacuum. They must meet the demands of the moral-cultural system and of the political system. While corporations spring from some of our most cherished ideals about liberty, initiative, investment in the future, cooperation, and the like, they must also be judged in the light of our ideals. They are moral-cultural institutions, as well as economic institutions. Their primary task is economic. One cannot ask them to assume crushing and self-destructive burdens. Yet they are more than economic organisms alone and must be held to political and moral judgment.

## Three Systems—Three Fields of Responsibility

The most original social invention of democratic capitalism, in sum, is the private corporation founded for economic purposes. The motivation for this invention was also social: to increase "the wealth of nations," to generate (for the first time in human history) sustained economic development. This effect was, in fact, achieved. However, the corporation—as a type of voluntary association—is not merely an economic institution. It is also a moral institution and a political institution. It depends upon and generates certain moral-cultural virtues; it depends upon and generates new political forms. In two short centuries, it has brought about an immense social revolution. It has moved the center of economic activity from the land to industry and commerce. No revolution is without social costs and sufferings, which must be entered on the ledger against benefits won. Universally, however, the idea of economic development has now captured the imagination of the human race. This new possibility of development has awakened the world from its economic slumbers.

Beyond its economic effects, the corporation changes the ethos and the cultural forms of society. To some extent, it has undercut ancient ways in which humans relate to each other, with some good effects and some bad. After the emergence of corporations, religion had to work upon new psychological realities. The religion of peasants has given way to the religion of new forms of life: first that of an urban proletariat, then that of a predominantly service and white-collar society. The productivity of the new economics has freed much human time for questions other than those of mere subsistence and survival. The workday has shrunk, and "weekends" have been invented. After work, millions now take part in voluntary activities that fill, in effect, another forty-hour week (associations, sports, travel, politics, religion, and the like). Personal and social mobility has increased. Schooling has become not only common but mandatory. Teenagerhood has been invented. The "stages of human life" have drawn attention with the emergence of the private self.

But the corporation is not only an economic institution and a moral-cultural institution: it also provides a new base for politics. Only a free political system permits the voluntary formation of private corporations. Thus, those who value private economic corporations have a strong interest in resisting both statism and socialism. It would be naive and wrong to believe that persons involved in corporations are (or should be) utterly neutral about political systems. An economic system within which private corporations play a role, in turn, alters the political horizon. It lifts the poor, creates a broad middle class, and undermines aristocracies of birth. Sources of power are created independent of the power of the state, in competition with the powers of the state, and sometimes in consort with the powers of the state. A corporation with plants and factories in, say, 120 congressional districts represents a great many employees and stockholders. On some matters, at least, they are likely to be well-organized to express their special political concerns. Political jurisdictions often compete to attract corporations; but their arrival also creates political problems.

Corporations err morally, then, in many ways. They may through their advertising appeal to hedonism and escape, in ways that undercut the restraint and self-discipline required by a responsible democracy and that discourage the deferral of present satisfaction on which savings and investment for the future depend. They may incorporate methods of governance that injure dignity, cooperation, inventiveness, and personal development. They may seek their own immediate interests at the expense of the common good. They may become improperly involved in the exercise of political power. They may injure the conscience of their managers or workers. They are capable of the sins of individuals and of grave institutional sins as well. Thus, it is a perfectly proper task of all involved within corporations and in society at large to hold them to the highest moral standards, to accuse them when they fail, and to be vigilant about every form of abuse. Corporations are human institutions designed to stimulate economic activism and thus to provide the economic base for a democratic polity committed to high moral-cultural ideals. When they fall short of these purposes, their failure injures all.

Private corporations are social organisms. Neither the ideology of laissez faire nor the ideology of rugged individualism suits their actual practice or their inherent ideals. For corporations socialize risk, invention, investment, production, distribution, and services. They were conceived and designed to break the immemorial grip of mercantilist and clerical systems upon economic activity. On the other hand, they cannot come into existence, and certainly cannot function, except within political systems designed to establish and to promote the conditions of their flourishing. Among these are a sound currency, a system of laws, the regulation of competitive practices, the construction of infrastructures like roads, harbors, airports, certain welfare functions, and the like. The state, then, plays an indispensable role in democratic capitalism. The ideals of democratic capitalism are not those of laissez faire. The relations between a democratic state and a social market economy built around private corporations are profound, interdependent, and complex.

The ideals of democratic capitalism are not purely individualist, either, for the corporation draws upon and requires highly developed social skills like mutual trust, teamwork, compromise, cooperation, creativity, originality and inventiveness, and agreeable management and personnel relations. The rugged individualist of an earlier mythology may be an endangered species.

Great moral responsibility, then, is inherent in the existence of corporations. They may fail economically. They may fail morally and culturally. They may fail politically. Frequently enough, they err in one or all these areas. They are properly subjected to constant criticism and reform. But types of criticism may be distinguished. Some critics accept the ideals inherent in the system of private business corporations, and simply demand that corporations be faithful to these ideals. Some critics are opposed to the system qua system. Among these, some wish to restrain, regulate, and guide the business system through the power of the state and/or through moral and cultural forces like public opinion, shame, ridicule, boycotts, and moral suasion ("do not invest in South Africa," for example). In the theory of "mixed systems," the ideal of democratic capitalism shades off into the ideal of democratic socialism—one leaning more to the private sector, the other leaning more to the public sector. Still other critics wish to make the business system directly subject to the state. These last may be, according to their own ideals, corporate statists or socialists. They may be state socialists or local participatory politics socialists. Criticism from any of these quarters may be useful to the development and progress of democratic capitalism, even from those who would wish to destroy it.

There is plenty of room—and plenty of evidence—for citing specific deficiencies of corporations: economic, political, and moral-cultural. To be sure, there is a difference between accusations and demonstrated error. Like individuals, corporations are innocent until proved guilty. A passionate hostility toward bigness (or even toward economic liberty), like a passionate commitment to statism, may be socially useful by providing a searching critique from the viewpoint of hostile critics. But unless it gets down to cases and sticks to a reasoned presentation of evidence, it must be recognized for what it is: an argument less against specifics than against the radical ideal of democratic capitalism and the private corporation. It is useful to distinguish these two types of criticism, and it is helpful when critics are self-conscious and honest about which ideals actually move them. To criticize corporations in the light of their own ideals, the ideals of democratic capitalism, is quite different from criticizing them in the name of statist or socialist ideals incompatible with their existence. Clarity about ideals is as necessary as clarity about cases.

Theologians, in particular, are likely to inherit either a pre-capitalist or a frankly socialist set of ideals about political economy. They are especially likely to criticize corporations from a set of ideals foreign to those of democratic capitalism. To those who do accept democratic-capitalist ideals, then, their criticisms are likely to have a scent of unreality and inappropriateness. Wisdom would suggest joining argument at the appropriate level of discourse—whether the argument concerns general economic concepts, whether it concerns the rival ideals of democratic capitalism and socialism, or whether it concerns concrete cases and specific matters of fact. Each of these levels has its place. Wisdom's principal task is *distinguer*.

Managing a free society aimed at preserving the integrity of the trinitarian system—the economic system, the political system, and the moral-cultural system—is no easy task. An important standard set by Edmund Burke is cited as the epigraph of a masterly work by Wilhelm T. Röpke, *A Humane Economy:*

> To make a government requires no great prudence. Settle the seat of power; teach obedience: and the work is done. To give freedom is still more easy. It is not necessary to guide; it only requires to let go the rein. But to form a *free government;* that is, to temper together these opposite elements of liberty and restraint in one consistent work, requires much thought, deep reflection, a sagacious, powerful and combining mind.[25]

[25] See Wilhelm T. Röpke, *A Humane Economy: The Social Framework of the Free Market* (Chicago: Henry Regnery, 1960), facing p. 1; the quotation is from Edmund Burke, *Reflections on the Revolution in France* (1790).

To govern a free economy is yet more difficult than to form a free government. It is hard enough to govern a government. It is difficulty squared to govern a free economy—to establish the conditions for prosperity, to keep a sound currency, to promote competition, to establish general rules and standards binding upon all, to keep markets free, to provide education to all citizens in order to give them opportunity, to care for public needs, and to provide succor to the unfortunate. To have the virtue to do all these things wisely, persistently, judiciously, aptly is surely of some rather remarkable theological significance. It may even represent—given the inherent difficulties—a certain amazing grace. To fall short is to be liable to judgment.

Christians have not, historically, lived under only one economic system; nor are they bound in conscience to support only one. Any real or, indeed, any imaginable economic system is necessarily part of history, part of this world. None is the Kingdom of Heaven—not democratic socialism, not democratic capitalism. A theology of the corporation should not make the corporation seem to be an ultimate; it is only a means, an instrument, a worldly agency. Such a theology should attempt to show how corporations may be instruments of redemption, of humane purposes and values, of God's grace; it should also attempt to show their characteristic and occasional faults in every sphere. Like everything else in the world, corporations may be seen as both obstacles to salvation and bearers of God's grace. The waters of the sea are blessed, as are airplanes and plowshares and even troops making ready for just combat. A city in Texas may be named Corpus Christi, and a city in California, Sacramento. Christianity, like Judaism, attempts to sanctify the real world as it is, in all its ambiguity, so as to reject the evil in it and bring the good in it to its highest possible fruition.

Most Christians do not now work for major industrial corporations. Instead, they work for the state (even in state universities), for smaller corporations, restaurants, barbershops, and other businesses. Still, a Christian social theology that lacks a theology of the large corporation will have no effective means of inspiring those Christians who do work within large corporations to meet the highest practicable Christian standards. It will also have no means of criticizing with realism and practicality those features of corporate life that deserve to be changed. Whether to treat big corporations as potential vessels of Christian vocation or to criticize them for their inevitable sins, Christian theology must advance much further than it has in understanding exactly and fairly every aspect of corporate life. The chief executive officer of General Electric needs such a theology. So do those critics of the corporation at the Interfaith Center for Corporate Responsibility. If we are to do better than clash like ignorant armies in the night, we must imitate Yahweh at Creation when he said, "Let there be light." We have not yet done all we should in casting such light.

# Bibliography

Barber, Richard J. *The American Corporation: Its Power, Its Money, Its Politics.* New York: E. P. Dutton, 1970.

Berle, Adolf A., Jr. *The Twentieth Century Capitalist Revolution.* New York: Harcourt, 1954.

Brozen, Yale; Mott, William C.; Tyrmand, Leopold; St. John, Jeffrey; Shenfield, Barbara; and Howard, John A. *Corporate Responsibility: The Viability of Capitalism in an Era of Militant Demands.* Rockford, Ill.: Rockford College Institute, 1978.

Davis, John P. *Corporations: A Study of the Origin and Development of Great Business Combinations and Their Relation to the Authority of the State.* 2 vols. New York: Putnam, 1961, reprint of 1905 edition.

Davis, Joseph S. *Essays in the Earlier History of American Corporations.* 2 vols. Cambridge, Mass.: Harvard University Press, 1917.

Drucker, Peter F. *Concept of the Corporation.* New York: John Day Co., 1946.

Finn, David. *The Corporate Oligarch.* New York: Simon & Schuster, 1969.

Frank, Isaiah. *Foreign Enterprise in Developing Countries.* Baltimore: Johns Hopkins University Press, 1980.

Galbraith, John Kenneth. *The New Industrial State.* Boston: Houghton Mifflin, 1967.

Hessen, Robert. *In Defense of the Corporation.* Stanford, Calif.: Hoover Institution Press, 1979.

Hewlitt, Sylvia Ann. *The Cruel Dilemmas of Development: Twentieth-Century Brazil.* New York: Basic Books, 1980.

Hunt, Bishop C. *The Development of the Business Corporation in England; 1800–1967.* Cambridge, Mass.: Harvard University Press, 1936.

Hurst, James Willard. *The Legitimacy of the Business Corporation in the Law of the United States, 1780–1970*. Charlottesville, Va.: University Press of Virginia, 1970.

Kristol, Irving. *Two Cheers for Capitalism*. New York: Basic Books, 1978.

Manne, Henry G., and Wallich, Henry C. *The Modern Corporation and Social Responsibility*. Washington, D.C.: American Enterprise Institute, 1972.

Moore, Wilbert E. *The Conduct of the Corporation*. New York: Random House, 1962.

Moran, T. H. *Multinational Corporations and the Politics of Dependence: Copper in Chile*. Princeton, N.J.: Princeton University Press, 1974.

Novak, Michael, and Cooper, John W., eds. *The Corporation: A Theological Inquiry*. Washington, D.C.: American Enterprise Institute, 1981.

Powers, Charles W. *Social Responsibility and Investment*. Nashville, Tenn.: Abingdon, 1971.

―――, and Vogel, David. *Ethics in the Education of Business Managers*. Hastings-on-Hudson, N.Y.: The Hastings Center, 1980.

Sigmund, Paul E. *Multinationals in Latin America: The Politics of Nationalization*. Madison, Wis.: University of Wisconsin Press, 1980.

Vernon, Raymond. *Sovereignty at Bay: The Multinational Spread of U.S. Enterprises*. New York: Basic Books, 1971.

Walton, Clarence. *The Ethics of Corporate Conduct*. Englewood Cliffs, N.J.: Prentice-Hall, 1977.

Williams, Oliver F., and Houck, John W. *Full Value: Cases in Christian Business Ethics*. New York: Harper & Row, 1978.